Praise for **one·mile·radius**

"Mark Deutschmann is one of Nashville's most creative thinkers. Both visionary and practical, his ideas on community revitalization, active transportation, energy conservation, and sustainable development are helping to transform Nashville. The ideas in *One-Mile Radius*, as well as Mark's leadership with both Greenways for Nashville and the Urban Land Institute, provide a guide to creating a better, more livable, more walkable city and region."

—**Ed McMahon,** senior resident fellow of Urban Land Institute

"Nashville has been a city on the rise for the last decade, and Mark Deutschmann has been at the forefront of helping to shape the growth and development that is ensuring our prosperity. I've had the pleasure of knowing Mark for many years, from when we first worked together to sell our home to now working with him on projects in the community to expand the supply of workforce housing so that our educators can live and work in the city where they teach.

Nashville has been fortunate to have Mark's leadership in driving the expansion of our Greenway network, which promotes sustainability while improving the quality of life for residents and adding value to nearby homes and businesses. As the mayor of Music City, it is important to have visionary partners in the community like Mark who understand that thoughtful planning and responsible development are in the best interest of the city they call home and their long-term financial success."

—**Megan Barry,** mayor of Nashville

"For twenty years, I've watched Mark work to create a progressive, neighborhood-based real estate firm that is one of Nashville's most successful community-minded companies. Mark is an inspiring entrepreneur with a thriving business that puts people and sense of place at its core."

—**Gregor Robertson,** mayor of Vancouver

"Our moment in history is marked by the triumph of the city. No one can help us understand this phenomenon like Mark Deutschmann. He is both scholar and practitioner, both visionary and street-level activist. His book, *One-Mile Radius*, is a book for our time."

—**Stephen Mansfield,** author and founder of the Mansfield Group

"In *One-Mile Radius*, Mark Deutschmann peels back the layers of his hugely successful business practices and socially driven endeavors to reveal the common denominator that drives his many passions—a profound love of Nashville. His efforts have been instrumental in transforming the city into a more walkable, vibrant, and connected place."

—**Gary Gaston,** executive director of the Nashville Civic Design Center

"Rare people do unusual things. When Mark Deutschmann launched what would become Village Real Estate and its development partners in Nashville, he thought in unusual time frames. It was about decades, not months, for that was how you'd affect the long term. He could see what needed to happen before others even sniffed out that there might be an opportunity, but it was the opportunity for building the sense of community, not primarily the bottom line, that gave vitality to what has become Village. It is the rare person that does the unusual thing.

To make this real, the company gave a percentage of itself to charity—the Village Fund at the Tides Foundation—before, not after it was a successful and profitable company. Village knew it wanted to help by doing more than building and selling great places to live; they wanted to create the reasons people would want to live in a place—a place that was a community of people, interests, culture, and roots. (You gotta have coffee and toilet paper within a short walk, no?) This is not what normal people do. Thank goodness there are the rare ones."

—**Drummond Pike,** founder and former CEO of the Tides Foundation and facilitator of Tides Canada

"In *One-Mile Radius*, Mark Deutschmann gives us a double dose of inspiration. First, he shows how his personal passion fueled not only a successful business but positive impacts in the world. Second, he invites us to consider our own communities and how each of us can play a part in making them better."

—**Elizabeth B. Crook,** CEO of Orchard Advisors, author of *Live Large: The Achiever's Guide to What's Next*

"Mark Deutschmann has walked and dreamed, built and sold, explored and juggled his way to a deep understanding of what a city needs and its people require. Mark knows and loves Nashville and his insights will move all who share that love here or anyplace else."

—**Bill Purcell,** former mayor of Nashville (1999–2007)

"As a developer, Mark understands a well-designed community genuinely connects people to a place and to each other to form the unique character and social fabric of a neighborhood, a city. As an entrepreneur, he recognizes the benefits of one's endeavors must spill over and filter, abundantly and deeply, into the community where you do business. And as a juggler capable of keeping so many balls synchronized in the air, Mark invites us to see the beautiful, rhythmic interconnectedness of seemly separate forces."

—**Renata Soto,** Conexión Américas co-founder & executive director

"Nashville is one of the most exemplary places to witness rapid urban and economic growth in America today. Living here makes one aware of how important issues of equity and health are in the design and governance of communities. Mark Deutschmann is a proven leader in Nashville for the way he designs communities through his real estate business and leads them through civic servitude and community organizing and partnerships. This book, Mark's thoughts on community, should be read by anyone looking to understand the principles and process for designing an exceptional one."

—**Marcus Whitney,** CEO and cofounder of Health: Further and founding partner of Jumpstart Foundry

"*One-Mile Radius* gives one a sneak peek at the incorrigible optimism and vision that Mark has for neighborhoods as places of social engagement, networks of meaningful open space and, ultimately, the healing and building of true community. Mark has always had the ability to habitually see things differently and to actively seek the beauty the dwells just beneath the surface. *One-Mile Radius* is an invitation to walk alongside Mark and share the journey."

—**Kim Hawkins,** cofounder and owner of Hawkins Partners, Inc.

"Mark Deutschmann is one of Nashville's most thoughtful business leaders. Mark has a genuine and successful commitment to sustainability, preservation of neighborhoods, alternative transportation, and the creation of a world-class greenway system. His new book is a needed contribution to the discussion of Nashville's dynamic future. Mark has already contributed so much to Nashville, and with this book he points the way to the future."

—**Karl Dean,** former mayor of Nashville

"Mark has tirelessly worked for the expansion of Greenways in Nashville. His creativity, dedication, and vision have not only increased the miles of Greenways in Nashville but also have led to enhanced public awareness and support for Greenways. His work is truly inspirational and has made our city a better place to live."

—**Anne Davis,** managing attorney at SELC, former first lady of Nashville, and board member of Greenways for Nashville

"Vancouver is a city that has always inspired me. I've enjoyed sharing that inspiration and a connection with my friend Mark Deutschmann as we supported each other and collaborated through the years to make both our cities (Vancouver and Nashville) healthier, greener, and more environmentally friendly. This book is a great manifestation of Mark's inspiration and charts a course for the role that business leaders can play in building vibrant communities."

—**Sadhu Aufochs Johnston,** city manager of Vancouver, British Columbia

"Mark personifies the soul of Hollyhock, where he first came searching for spirit and meaning and a way to incorporate those into his young real estate business. He is an inspired leader who pours passion and vision into strengthening his business and his community. We are honored to be part of his story and have him as part of ours."

—**Dana Bass Solomon,** CEO of Hollyhock

"At Hands On Nashville, Mark's vision and leadership and his Go Green program inspired the Home Energy Savings program. It continues to impact thousands of Nashvillians by improving energy efficiency and reducing utility and home maintenance costs so seniors and low-income families can continue living in their neighborhoods."

—**Brian Williams,** former CEO of Hands On Nashville

"In the late 1990s, I worked with Mark, neighbors, and merchants on the revitalization of the 12South neighborhood commercial district. We overcame significant negative 'conventional wisdom,' mistrust, inertia, and bad infrastructure to create a place where folks now shop, play, and work in their neighborhood without getting into a car. It was a proud day when we cut the ribbon on the 'new edition' of 12South!"

—**Phil Ryan,** Metro Development and Housing Agency Nashville, 1991–2013

"How can I count the ways Mark has left his 'mark' on this city we love? Many would say the idea of modern 'urban living' was an oxymoron before Mark applied his special magic to knitting our communities together: the literal community as he led the way to build 'villages' in our city; sustainable communities as he spearheaded energy efficiency; irresistible communities as he drove our acceleration of greenways; and engaged communities as he modeled and led corporate philanthropy to give to our greenways to tie our city together. Not to mention he established a company fund that has given to and celebrated dozens of nonprofits. These are the marks of his fingerprints using only one hand. The counting goes on, and this book is one more generous gift of inspiration to all of us."

—**Jeanie Nelson,** founder of the Land Trust for Tennessee

"Today, Nashville is a more vibrant, more beautiful, and healthier city thanks to the unrelenting efforts of Mark Deutschmann. Mark has made a lasting imprint across our community through his altruistic works, vision, and activism. Mark is a naturally holistic thinker and a straightforward, focused problem solver. His passion and his 'can-do' approach motivates others . . . a sign of a true leader. Mark's perspective on Nashville and how a city can flourish is sure to inspire."

—**Hunter Gee,** principle at Smith Gee Studio, LLC

"*One-Mile Radius* gives a glimpse inside the world of real estate as it should be practiced. Real estate agents are portals to the greater community and mastering this leads to personal fulfillment, solid relationships, and income that can sustain well beyond the average agent's tenure. No one can tell this story of mastery better than Mark Deutschmann."

—**Brian Copeland,** president of the Tennessee Association of REALTORS

"Mark is an unusual entrepreneur with strong, seemingly equal passions for both development and green quality of life. As a business leader and environmentalist he effectively champions and fully understands the benefits of both interests and how they help each other. He puts his high energy as well as resources into stimulating transformative civic improvements.

As a member of Nashville's Greenways Commission and president of the nonprofit friends group, Greenways for Nashville, Mark put his sharp sales acumen to work and elevated community-wide spirit for green spaces and trails. Among the first developers locally to embrace and advance the concept of greenways for trail-oriented development, Mark hits the mark to connect the dots literally and figuratively, from place-making, open space, and the environment, to economic development."

—**Shain Dennison,** assistant director of Metro Parks, Greenways and Open Space Division

"Mark's love and understanding of the city he chose as his place in the world, combined with his keen ability to envision its potential, masterfully shows us the way toward building vibrant communities—the places we all yearn to live in. Read this book and learn lessons in place-making and the role that local businesses can play in building just, sustainable, and community-based economies in your own region. In these challenging times of climate change, this book shows how urban life can lower carbons and increase both resilience and happiness. Mark's love of life is infectious; the joy of community leaps from these pages!"

—**Judy Wicks,** author of *Good Morning, Beautiful Business* and cofounder of the Business Alliance for Local Living Economies

"In Mark's formative years of reflection and spiritual development, I witnessed his dedicated sincerity in plumbing the depth of innate questioning to a vibrant understanding of interconnection. From forging skill in interpersonal relating to walking with the indigenous peoples of Peru, Mark's spirit of inclusivity became the basis of his work in the community and in the world. Mark's story invites us to partake in living wisdom and compassion."

—**Roshi Sanchi Reta Lawler,** Zen Buddhist teacher

one · mile · radius

one · mile · radius

Building community from the core

MARK DEUTSCHMANN

Advantage®

Published by Advantage, Charleston, South Carolina.
Member of Advantage Media Group.

ADVANTAGE is a registered trademark, and the Advantage colophon is a trademark of Advantage Media Group, Inc.

Printed in the United States of America.

10 9 8 7 6 5 4 3 2

ISBN: 978-1-59932-536-1
LCCN: 2017940503

Cover and layout design by George Stevens.

To Nashville, for welcoming me and growing with me.

❧

All proceeds from this book go to the Village Fund, a nonprofit foundation and charitable arm of Village Real Estate Services that provides grants to organizations helping to enrich and strengthen our neighborhoods. The Village Fund focuses on four areas of giving: housing, community, environment & smart growth and the arts.

SALEMTOWN
65
1
GERMANTOWN
440
DOWNTO
NASHVIL
THE
NATIONS
THE GULCH
5
SYLVAN
PARK
7
WEDGEWOOD-HOUSTO
HILLSBORO
VILLAGE
6
RICHLAND
CENTRAL
8
12SOUTH
440
2
GREEN HILLS

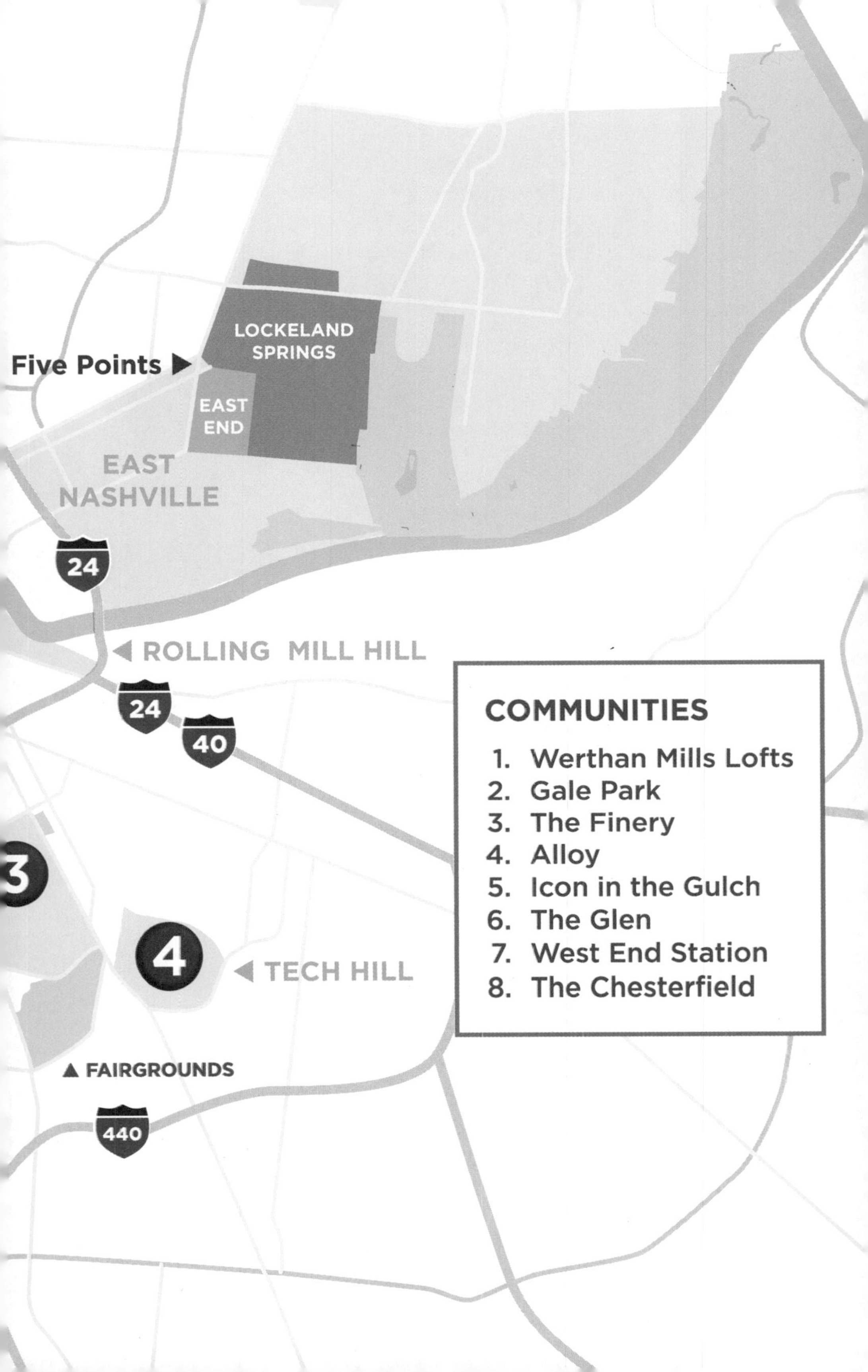
LOCKELAND SPRINGS
Five Points
EAST END
EAST NASHVILLE
24
ROLLING MILL HILL
24
40
3
4
TECH HILL
FAIRGROUNDS
440
COMMUNITIES
1. Werthan Mills Lofts
2. Gale Park
3. The Finery
4. Alloy
5. Icon in the Gulch
6. The Glen
7. West End Station
8. The Chesterfield

Table of Contents

Foreword

MARK'S TINY BOAT limped along for hours, half sailing, half drifting on the swift Blackfish Sound waters toward the ocean just to the north of Vancouver Island. His boat's motor had crapped out, leaving him with no alternative but to rig up a sail from scrounged materials and hope he would not be pushed by the wind and tides out to the open ocean.

At the time, I was in my midtwenties and acting as caretaker for the killer whale research laboratory on Hanson Island, forty-five minutes by powerboat from the First Nations village of Alert Bay. As the only two authorized human residents of the island, my girlfriend and I built gardens, fed the dogs, and explored the island all summer. It was exhilarating, though a bit lonely. The profound landscape had dynamic sixteen-foot tides, powerful currents, dense forests, a strong native culture, and an active orca feeding ground. Orcas, known to the local First Nations residents as blackfish and more commonly known as killer whales, came to feast on salmon returning from their multiyear journeys from far out to sea back to their birth rivers to spawn.

That was where I first met Mark. He simply walked into our campsite, exhausted and grateful to be off the ocean and alive. All these years later, my beloved friend and business partner still has that daring, charm, and love of adventure that quickly won over two complete strangers in a matter of minutes.

Some years later I moved to Nashville in Davidson County, Tennessee, where my father, Jay Solomon, had restarted his real estate development business. Mark came to visit shortly after my dad died in 1984, as I was starting to manage the family business with my sister, Linda Solomon, and longtime associate Martha Burton.

Mark instantly fell for Nashville's friendly atmosphere and budding opportunities and decided to stay. He was a relentless entrepreneur in those early years as he worked to gain his foothold. He began as a window washer (having no worries about reaching far from tall ladders), and then he busked as a juggler; he could generate a crowd in a flash. He even sold futons by posting ads on light poles, bringing potential customers to see his futon in his home, ordering one for them from the factory, and shipping it to their front door a few days later—at a decent markup, of course.

We shared a big four-square in Belmont Hillsboro that I bought for $140,000 in the late 1980s. I overpaid in what was a declining neighborhood at the time but which has since reawakened thanks to visionaries such as Gene and Penny Teselle, who were early neighborhood leaders. After work, we used to walk for hours through the wonderful, early twentieth-century neighborhoods of the university zone of Nashville. We were learning the lay of the land and the wonders of a well-created community.

Mark and I have this insatiable curiosity when it comes to Nashville, and we love experiencing each new greenway the city builds. I served on the board of the early Greenways Commission, but it was during Mark's tenure in this organization, over twenty years later, that greenways really flourished in Nashville. We still talk for hours and hours. It's Mark's love for and dedication to the Nashville community that makes him so effective at everything he does. It also makes this book a colorful, creative, and very meaningful tale of how building a business the right way is good for a community, its people, and the natural world that supports it all.

I've since moved to the visionary city of Vancouver, returning to that captivating region of my twenties. I have taken the lessons that I learned with Mark in our many business ventures and live our "one-mile radius" mentality every day.

This is a unique story about an entrepreneur who knows how to use business as a powerful tool for positive community and cultural change. His vision is infectious and inspires forward-thinking, progressive, political leadership and the celebration of neighborhoods and communities.

His boundless passion and commitment could not have come at a better time for Nashville. He writes about a crucial era in the city's history when the city almost lost its historic neighborhoods. Instead, with the work and vision of people like Mark, those neighborhoods have become the envy of cities across the nation. Nashville has demonstrated how thriving small businesses, jobs, prosperity, and smarter citizens model the creative economy that will fuel much of the future of urban life.

Mark's tale is far more than wonderful business stories. It's about how authenticity, strong values, forward vision, and true caring about people and the planet can change the future.

Give Mark a chance to share his experiences with you, as I did all of those years ago when he walked into my campsite. You'll be glad you did.

—***Joel Solomon,*** *author of* Clean Money Revolution
and board chair of Renewal Funds

Introduction

I STARTED PRACTICING real estate in Nashville, Tennessee, in 1986 and opened my own real estate company in 1996. Village Real Estate Services, known today as Village, is now in its twenty-first year and has grown to include nearly 350 agents and staff. Collectively, and over time, our work has had an effect on the complexion of the city. When I started, urban neighborhoods were not thriving, and the neighborhood commercial districts were underused. We were at the end of the era of "urban flight," the result of the proliferation of car-oriented development trends. It was not a pretty version of our city.

Along the way, I realized that to be truly successful in growing any real estate business, you have to be both a good real estate practitioner and a community builder. That's what this book is about. By connecting residential neighborhoods back to the city's very core, I was able to add value to communities in the heart of Nashville with the aim of making them the most vibrant, sustainable, walkable places they could be. I focused my work on the ring neighborhoods, the first trolley car "suburbs" built in the 1920s and 1930s, and on our inner neighborhood commercial districts. I liked to say that "the core is the new edge"—it's a movement that understands that everyone craves community and wants to live in neighborhoods where people can walk, gather, and commune. Though there is an enduring appeal to the suburbs, that doesn't need to be at the expense of some of the great neighborhoods in our city.

This effort has, over many years, resulted in what I have come to call the "one-mile radius" effect, a positive wave of impact that builds momentum neighborhood by neighborhood. I began to see that each neighborhood has its own identity—its own unique commercial corners, natural features, politics, and collection of players and leaders. Once we have a good sense of a neighborhood, we can bring in the right infrastructure, development, programming, marketing, and connection to recreate and enhance what already exists.

Our goal has always been to support the influential role that cities have on human innovation and creativity. It's this positive wave of evolution in our inner neighborhoods that causes many creative people to prefer the city to the suburbs. It is no accident that humans across the planet are migrating toward cities and to the dynamic core of their communities. They, like me, crave a local living economy.

I'm also a firm believer that cities create the most environmentally friendly conditions for human existence and, as report after report confirms, that humans have severely impacted the changing climate. By recreating core neighborhoods with infrastructure, density on our corridors, walkability, and urban greening initiatives, we are reducing our carbon footprint, slowing sprawl, and saving resources on the planet. We just have one planet, and by creating strong communities we can make a positive contribution toward preserving it.

Furthermore, urban living can be healthy. Strong neighborhood commercial districts, coupled with good public transportation and greenways, promote walking, which is key in bettering our collective health. Nashville is a health care community, with one of the strongest health care business sectors in the country. Our health care community would be well served to pay better attention and to give more support to conditions that better urban living and a healthy citizenry.

I also began to understand that the key to successful neighborhood development is in partnerships. I saw that there are some amazing initiatives just waiting to be tapped and partners who are eager to invest in our community. Partnerships created my own success, and they also create Nashville's success. I have partnered with social profit organizations, such as the Nashville Civic Design Center (NCDC), Hands On Nashville (HON), Nashville Downtown Partnership (NDP), the Nashville chapter of the Urban Land Institute (ULI), Entrepreneurs' Organization (EO), and Greenways for Nashville (GfN). I have founded social profit and for-profit companies including Village Real Estate Services, the Village Fund, Go Green, 1221 Partners, Solve, Core Development, and the City-Living Group, my personal sales team at Village. I have worked with all of these entities to help Nashville recreate thriving communities where people are attracted to live, work, and play.

Other partners and influences that have allowed me to build community include the Social Venture Network; Hollyhock; the Nashville Juggling Club; Scattered Showers; my wife, Sherry Stewart Deutschmann, and her work with her company, LetterLogic; my longtime friend Joel Solomon; the agents and staff of my own companies; and, of course, my family.

This focus with partners on community development and on the stewardship of our environment creates what is happening in that one-mile radius, and I will be sharing stories and ideas in this book that will support this thesis. I will also explore some of these questions: How does urban density work, and where should it be in our city? Do we need a strong platform to create an environmentally friendly city? How do we provide housing and studios to preserve our creative class? How can we embrace our emerging immigrant community? What is "too much" development, and what should we do about it? Should our health care community embrace the emerging greenway system to help solve Nashville's poor health rankings? We are at a turning point, when we have to choose whether we should care about these things or not.

I've learned a lot along my journey, both in work and in play, and I hope my experiences will help spark your passion and curiosity to get involved in your own community and to consider what you can do in your one-mile radius.

Chapter 1

Nightwalks

Deep in us, we know that the transformation of a city is dependent on transformed people and that finally a commitment to the building of the city has to involve a commitment to change in us.

—Elizabeth O'Connor,
Our Many Selves

WHEN PEOPLE ASK me how I came to Nashville, I often reply, "My boat engine caught on fire."

This simple, life-changing mishap occurred in 1982, during my second year working on a study of orcas, also known as killer whales. Jeff Jacobsen had been studying orcas for years, and I met him when I was an undergrad pursuing Spanish and zoology degrees at

Humboldt State University in Arcata, California. Jeff was based in Arcata, working on a doctorate, and for seven years he'd been studying the northern community of orcas. During the summer months, 150 or so whales of this community come to the Johnstone Strait, taking up residence in this protected waterway between Vancouver and the Canadian mainland.

Mark observing orcas in Johnstone Strait.

I spent much of my time on a twelve-foot Zodiac in essentially an inflatable tube with an engine. At the end of my second season, in mid-September of 1982, I was headed to Alert Bay with all of my gear, ready to jump into my 1972 Chevy Blazer to make the thousand-mile drive back down to Arcata. That's when I came upon a superpod of killer whales, a mixing of various pods in a large group—in this case, about twenty-five to thirty of them. They were going my way at a slow, playful speed, and I set my Zodiac to pace them and climbed over my stuff to my bow, leaning over to be near them.

After a while, however, I looked back and realized with surprise that my engine was smoking, and sure enough, I had a fire. Apparently a plastic bag had been sucked into the intake, and I had not noticed that the engine was slowly overheating. Before I could do anything, the engine died, and I was adrift. The orcas moved on and I watched them go. With the tide against me, and with no propulsion, I started to drift out toward the sea. This, of course, was a time before cell phones, and I did not have a radio. Uh-oh.

I did, luckily, have a windsurfer with a sail.

I opened it, secured it to the boat, stood on my seat, and sailed my little boat up the strait. I battled tidal rips, dodged large vessels in the sea lane, and finally landed on Hanson Island nine hours later, exhausted. Little did I know at the time that this harrowing journey was truly charting the course for the waters ahead.

When I walked into the camp, I found a long-bearded, long-haired, barefoot man named Joel Solomon and his hippie girlfriend, Louise Bracewell. They were the caretakers and sole inhabitants of the camp, and I was grateful they were there. Over the next seven days, I fished and foraged with Joel and sang and chatted with Louise. We became so close that I visited them again the next year after my final year of whale research. Joel and Louise had moved to another island, Cortes, about eighty miles south, and I arrived during the harvest season. Without the mishap, I may never have met Joel, and my life (and possibly even Nashville) would have likely turned out very differently.

Even though I had to deal with hazardous situations like fire and other mishaps in the wilderness, I enjoyed my research experience with the orcas because I collaborated with many international research teams. It was these collaborations that spurred me to enroll in the Thunderbird School of Global Management MBA program in 1983. I was better suited as a businessman than a scientist, and my enjoyment of collaboration was a forebear to my interest in partnerships. My studies kept me busy, but the attraction to Cortes Island didn't stop. After my first year of the MBA, I went back in the summer of 1984 and spent a season at Hollyhock, a not-for-profit lifelong learning and leadership center. There I learned the triple bottom line business model—businesses that work not just to spin a profit, but also to give back to people and the planet as a whole. I worked thirty hours per week at Hollyhock for room, board, and access to programs. I mostly worked outside on that amazing land, clearing trails, building fences, gardening, and doing other menial chores.

In April 1985 I was completing my MBA and interviewing for positions with international firms when my life took an unexpected turn. My mother called on the morning of April 13 to let me know that my father had died of a heart attack at fifty-four years of age. It was a great shock for my family and me. My father had been the undisputed patriarch in our family and a pillar in the community. Over the years I had distanced myself from him to find my own way. Now that he had passed away, my instinctive reaction was that I, as the eldest son, must find my place and begin to assert myself in both my family and in my career. Perhaps my father's death was part of the catalyst for what would come next. In May I finished my degree and moved back to Maryland to help my mother sell the family home.

That summer I got a call from Joel. Coincidentally, his father had also died, and he was in Nashville settling his family's estate. I came to Nashville to visit him in October and instantly felt an affinity for the community that he'd established. He had a very active household and was engaged in meaningful endeavors. Following the course I'd set years before when I shipwrecked my Zodiac, I made the snap decision to move to Nashville. Joel's father and family had been shopping mall developers, among other things, and had various real estate assets, so I got a real estate license as soon as I could to help out. Quite a distance from international business and orcas!

I was craving both core and community. Perhaps it was my time of life or I was hungry for meaning. I needed to find myself, and for me community was central. Perhaps we come to our greatest achievements, our greatest offers, by offering what we ourselves need. Returning Nashville to its core as a robust, healthy city mirrored my

Mark juggling pumpkins at a Franklin Halloween Festival in his early days.

return to my own core. I had also at this time in life become a serious juggler, and I was looking for opportunities to hone my craft.

Joel's dad had an office downtown in the St. Cloud Corner building, at the corner of Fifth and Church. This is the building that now houses Puckett's Grocery (and is at the corner of two streets where Core Development, my development entity, years later developed four projects). I'd go downtown to work out of the office, even though I didn't really have a job, and was struck by how cold and empty the streets felt, particularly on nights and weekends. The city's policies, which had emphasized the central commercial district at the expense of residential, had taken a toll. This was just a few years before the last retail outlets, such as Cain-Sloan and Castner Knott, closed shop and well before the age of real downtown neighborhoods.

On top of that, most of the commercial districts and adjacent neighborhoods were victims of urban flight, including Hillsboro Village, the 12South district, the funky neighborhoods in East Nashville with a mix of races and generations, and corner commercial corridors with unrealized potential to serve the community. Many had become dotted with ugly in-fill duplexes as lots were purchased by absentee landlords after the older homes collapsed. At this time, the neighborhood commercial districts in our ring neighborhoods were the closest things that we had to a community building core. It would be years before we moved back to fully recapture the heart of our city.

At the time, I was not attracted to the commercial sales side of the business, but I loved the neighborhood commercial districts. I was passionate about the older, transitional neighborhoods—such as Hillsboro Village, filled with old homes of character, which had fared better than our commercial and retail downtown and much better than some of the other less fortunate urban neighborhoods because of its proximity to Vanderbilt. It had a couple of taverns, a pet shop called Fido, a shoe repair shop, Patsy and Fayes, and the old Pancake Pantry, but the merchants were not well-organized and didn't do much to promote themselves.

I'm a night owl, and Joel and I often went out late in the evenings for walks. We walked the streets and alleyways, learning about our neighborhood through the lens of the night. While we walked through Hillsboro Village and the West End to Twelfth Avenue South, we talked about reinhabiting urban neighborhoods and the general patterns of renovation and revitalization. Downtown was essentially devoid of any activity, other than the homeless and the night workers. Nashville had not yet decided to allow residential development in the core, and we might not have gotten to know our city so well if we hadn't walked it.

Joel and I drew sustenance from our urban night ramblings and our midnight hikes in the city's green spaces. If you are in real estate, it's easy to forget the green spaces exist, but they are the quiet breath of the city landscape. In Nashville, our favorite refuge was Radnor Lake State Park, a 1,332-acre protected natural area located in Oak Hill, unique because of the abundance of wildlife, environmental education programs, hiking, and location in an urban area. The park is day-use only and there are more than six miles of trail. We loved to break the rules and hike Radnor Lake at night, sneaking in and walking the lake trail and hiking the ridges. Only once did a ranger with a flashlight tell us to turn back. We always wondered if he was one of the rangers we knew by day who recognized us and chose not to bust us. We were both big supporters of Friends of Radnor Lake, and we certainly meant no harm. We were getting to know all parts of the city so that we could learn what it offered, what it needed, and how it could be served.

We called our explorations "nightwalks," as they gave us the time needed to do some big-picture thinking. One of the keys to big-picture thinking is to get rid of all distractions. In this day and age, that especially means screens (we need to choose our distractions wisely). While I know it sounds extreme, walking in the dark actually spurs incredible creativity. In the dark you have to focus on the next step, and without good vision, brain activity is heightened, allowing for an extraordinary pathway to new ideas and innovation.

During these walks, we formulated our philosophies about money and business and came up with concepts such as interdependent independence, how to be attentive but released in relationship to money, and how to find work/life integration. With money, for instance, we asked, how much is enough? Why? What then? Money, when aligned with positive long-term outcomes, could be a force for good. We often thought about the concept of "stepping in front of the parade" and our role in furthering trends in the city. We imagined the future that we wanted to create, with the quality of positive attitude, and pledged to seek wise council and to continue our personal development. These nightwalks were the foundation in developing my own philosophy around what I wanted to bring to the table in real estate, including my value in seeding a vibrant core, central to a city's health.

Around this time, I had a four-year stint with Renaissance Real Estate Company, run by Andy Allen and headquartered on Woodland Street in East Nashville. In those early days, I discovered satisfaction in connecting people to homes in emerging urban communities. Recalling early sales, I used the MLS book, which came out every two weeks—the precursor to the electronic version—to choose the listings that I would show my buyers. When the book came in, I would quickly open to the new listings in the back to see if any were a match for my customers. To show a property, I'd call the office of the listing agent, because we had no agent-showing service back then. Then I'd go to their office to pick up the keys. There were no electronic lockboxes at that time. I'd show the homes, hoping I had picked the right homes for my customer because there were no cell phones and no Internet, making it more difficult to shift a showing schedule on the fly. When I was done, I had to get all of the keys back to the corresponding offices. And I'd have to answer calls from agents to give them feedback. This was way before online feedback.

If my customers wanted to make an offer, we'd get together and write it up by hand—you got it, no electronic signatures—and I'd deliver it to the listing agent. If we got into negotiations, we'd deliver contracts back and forth for initials until the deal was done. The inspector required me to meet them to unlock the home for inspection, as did the appraiser, which meant getting and returning the keys once again. The good news for agents, perhaps, is that the only way a customer could find listings was by driving by signs in the yard or by reading print ads in the local paper. I had a good *Nashville Scene* presence at the time, having launched a clever campaign with unique print ads, designed by Miriam Myers, to showcase my growing listing pool within a one-mile radius of Hillsboro Village.

Ah, how the game has changed, with Internet, apps, key systems, showing systems, real estate search engines, online advertising, contact management systems, and such. But in many ways it's still the same, with an emotional buyer searching for their dream and an emotional seller making a life transition, working with us to come together in a home sale. That is the pattern that connects in our industry and always will.

During those early years, Andy taught me the joy of helping people find homes while working with them in a more holistic way to enhance their communities. This meant working through the challenge of securing financing for those who had little cash and meeting the challenge of homes that required significant repairs in order to secure bank financing. I relished the challenge, saw many people get homes who had not been able to do so before, and witnessed neighborhoods improving one house at a time. I really came to believe in the American Dream of home ownership, and I could see firsthand how those who own homes generally fare better economically than those who rent.

And I saw how pride of ownership effectively altered neighborhoods. You could see change happening home by home and block by block. The often maligned keeping-up-with-the-Joneses syndrome also created a positive scenario where one home renovation affected an entire street, producing a remarkable transformation. After seeing what had happened in the core of the city, where older homes had fallen apart due to deferred maintenance, this neighborhood transformation was a joy to witness.

At Renaissance, Andy required his agents to define their geographic territories. I chose the territory bounded by Belmont Boulevard and West End but also asked for and received permission to work the neighborhood commercial district along Twelfth Avenue South, even though it ran through the residential territory of another Renaissance agent, Trasbin Stoner.

That's how I began to work within a one-mile radius of Hillsboro Village, where so many nights I had walked with Joel. Word spread that this was my niche. The Hillsboro Village neighborhoods, in progressively worse shape as you moved east, had been ravaged by suburban flight and redlining. There was no active merchant association in the Hillsboro Village commercial district and too many absentee landlords in the neighborhoods.

It is tremendously important as a real estate agent to show your clients that you understand their area of interest and to prove that you are invested in it. Because of those night walks, I knew what I was in for. By choosing a specific niche, you are showing clients what is unique and different about you—what sets you apart from all the others. It's something they will remember when they are in a position to refer other clients. The niche can be geographical, or it can focus on a particular buyer type. If you simply say, "I'm a real estate agent," you may not be memorable. When people asked me what I did, I said, "I sell real estate within a one-mile radius of Hillsboro Village." This was my unique selling proposition (USP) that I used to acquire a core group of clients in an area I knew the best.

Generally, people responded with "That's all you do?"

"Yes, but I know every home on the market, every home coming on the market, and everything about these homes," I replied. "I know that people are looking to be near this emerging commercial district. If anyone you know wants to live near Hillsboro Village, please let me know, and I'll be sure to help them."

Though this was perceived as quirky, the strategy worked. I quickly discovered the power of dedicating my time and efforts to a small geographic zone and how that can translate to expertise, which then impacts the direction of a neighborhood. Now when people thought about Hillsboro Village they thought of Mark Deutschmann. If anyone was aligned with this neighborhood and wanted to relocate there, they were directed to me. This was my core. Having a core worked well for both me and my burgeoning customer base, and I was able to sell them homes and plug them into my growing community. Soon I was the top agent with the most listings in the area and was able to use my influence to positively effect change.

This was where the triple bottom line came in. I wasn't just turning a profit, I was helping to revitalize a dying area and therefore the community, city, state, and economy at the same time. These were the days when people moving back to the city were viewed as urban pioneers. They were tired of the commute and wanted to live closer to where they worked. We had over forty-five thousand jobs downtown, but most of the workers were commuting from the suburbs. Our urban neighborhoods were in decline with homes that had been rentals for years, many of which were in dire need of renovation. Redevelopment of urban neighborhoods into mixed-use areas with denser residential development and eclectic commercial space was at that time foreign to a city council that mainly presided over Nashville's suburbanization.

As I worked to make the neighborhood surrounding this commercial district more attractive, and facilitated purchases and renovations on every street, the streetscapes and facades became steadily more attractive. Young families and empty nesters began moving back to Nashville from outlying suburbs. They were looking for neighborhoods with walkability, classic old homes—livable communities. Now a long way from Hanson Island and the orcas, I prepared to help Nashville change.

The late 1980s and early 1990s were those formative years in my real estate career and in developing my connection to Nashville. Living and working in Nashville's urban neighborhoods, I likely saw more "character" than real estate agents who were working the suburbs. Some of my earlier memories include work with the "Farmies."

In 1971, a caravan of eighty white school buses carrying 320 hippie idealists had followed Stephen and Ina May Gaskin from San Francisco and landed in Summertown, Tennessee. With a dream to create an intentional community, and with their pooled resources, they had realized that their funds would buy only fifty acres in California. In Summertown they bought 1,064 acres and established The Farm.

In the earliest days, members took vows of poverty and had no personal possessions. Farm members did not use birth control, drink alcohol, or use tobacco products, and abortion was prohibited. The Farm publicly offered to deliver any baby for free and to find a loving family to raise the child. Childbearing was natural, and births were attended by midwives. Ina May wrote the book *Spiritual Midwifery,* and her teachings and travels led to a later and somewhat coincidental meeting at Hollyhock when she and Stephen visited to do a workshop.

The Farm's outreach led to a population boom that peaked at around 1,600 members. The community's infrastructure could not support its members and went through a de-collectivization called "the changeover," requiring the members to support themselves with their own income. The rural surroundings did not offer much opportunity, so many members lived and worked in Nashville, where they started small businesses, invested in the city, and bought homes. I sold quite a number of homes to these "Farmies" in the emerging urban neighborhoods.

I also had quite a number of creatives as buyers, including many in the arts who were attracted to the character and low price points of homes in our emerging neighborhoods. Denice Hicks and Bruce Arntson, married at the time, were early clients, buying a house near Sevier Park. Denice was an original company member of the Tennessee Repertory Theatre and among the founders of Darkhorse Theater and of People's Branch Theatre. She has been working with the Nashville Shakespeare Festival since 1990 as an actor, director, and teaching artist and holds the title of artistic director. So prevalent is her influence that she is considered the "face" of Nashville theater.

Bruce is an actor, composer, and writer, and at the time he was working on a series of projects with director Coke Sams. Both he and Denice acted in the Ernest series with Jim Varney. This hilarious series, which featured Jim in the character of Ernest P. Worrell, included some wacky shows, starting with *Hey Vern, It's Ernest,* a 1988 children's television series. Bruce and Denice were Mike the Clown and Mrs. Clown, and Bruce was Existo the Magician. This led to a couple of movies: *Ernest Goes to Jail* in 1990 and *Ernest Goes to School* in 1994. Later, in 1999, Bruce starred in *Existo*, expanding on the character he'd developed. More recently, Bruce has been starring in the *Doyle and Debbie Show*—his creation—a spoof on country music. You can catch him down at the Station Inn in the Gulch.

Given that Music Row is within a one-mile radius of Hillsboro Village, I also worked with many writers and musicians. The writers in Nashville are at the heart of the music business—really the reason we are known as Music City. Many of them chose to buy houses in the neighborhood. I would sell them homes, then go watch them sing their songs, often the hits of the big-name entertainers, "in the round"—a Nashville tradition—at the bars and clubs. Vanderbilt and Belmont University were also in the neighborhood, and I worked with many professors and academicians. Nashville has another name—the Athens of the South—because we have so many universities, and perhaps because we have a life-size replica of the Parthenon in Centennial Park.

I loved working with unusual people, and I was always looking for innovative and creative ways to extend and expand my business. I studied with some of the top producers in the nation, including Ralph Roberts, an agent in Michigan who was selling six hundred homes per year at that time with his team. I'd read his book, *Walk Like a Giant, Sell Like a Madman,* and noted that *Time* magazine called him "the best-selling Realtor in America." Ralph allowed an agent to shadow him for a fee, meaning that I could tag along with him throughout the day. I went to his meetings and listing and sales appointments and spent some time with his staff. Ralph was a big, jovial extrovert who loved people and thrived on the art of the deal. Years later, I can't really remember what I learned that I actually put into practice, but I do remember that Ralph loved my juggling and that he made me juggle for each of the clients he met that day to help him close the deal. I should have charged him for my performance.

I also studied with Craig Proctor, a real estate agent and sales coach up in Toronto who billed himself as the top-selling agent in the worldwide ReMax system. He taught the Quantum Leap System ("Seven breakthrough real estate technologies that will change your game"). One thing that I implemented was the "ten-minute home tour." Instead of the traditional open house, I invited the public to view seven homes in one afternoon. This worked for me because I had a lot of clustered listings within that one-mile radius. I put pointers up throughout the neighborhood, and the signs in front of the homes read "Open House, 2:30–2:40 p.m.," "Open House, 2:45–2:55 p.m.," and so on, ending with the last home "Open House, 3:50–4 p.m." I would rent a fifteen-seat van and invite buyers to ride with me to see all of the homes. I had another agent leapfrog the van, staying in front and readying each open house. There were always people lining up to see each house, particularly when I added new listings. We pulled up in the van, and everyone came in. The ten-minute opening with lots of people created a lot of excitement, which generated lots of offers.

Another tactic Craig recommended was "If I can't sell your home in ninety days, I'll buy it." It was gimmicky, required an advance contract with a seller, and contained some special stipulations. I put my first ad in the *Nashville Scene* and waited for the calls to come in. At the time, I had a big old house on the market, built in 1907 and one of the originals. It was painted pink with baby blue trim, and had, by my count, twenty-eight major flaws. The home had been on the market for a year as each potential buyer bailed at the inspection. As it goes, that seller set my ad down in front of me and said, "It's been over ninety days." I reeled and let her know that there were some stipulations to consider. She demanded to hear about the whole program, and I gave her the "number." She said, "I'll take it."

I bought the home and nipped that offer in the bud. My wife and I still live in that home today.

Given that I was working with creatives, I came across the Cultural Creatives, a term coined by Paul Ray in 1995 and that influenced my thinking and business. In 2000 Ray followed with the book *The Cultural Creatives: How 50 Million People Are Changing the World.* He describes Cultural Creatives as a large segment of Western civilization who, since about 1985, have developed beyond the standard paradigm of progressives versus traditionalists. He divides them into two types. The Core Cultural Creatives, who are the more educated, leading-edge thinkers, a category that includes many writers, artists, musicians, psychotherapists, and so on. This group has a serious focus on spirituality and a passion for social activism. The other type, the Green Cultural Creatives, tends to follow the opinions of the Core group and has a more conventional religious outlook.

That said, both of these groups have common characteristics, including love of nature, strong awareness of planetary issues, remaining active, and being willing to pay more for goods or higher taxes if improving the environment. They emphasize the importance of developing and maintaining relationships and helping others; volunteer for one or more good causes; see spirituality as an important aspect of life and worry about religious fundamentalism; desire equity for women and men in business, life, and politics; are unhappy with left and right politics; have an optimism about the future; and are involved in creating a new and better way of life. Their values include authenticity, actions that are consistent with words and beliefs, engaged action and whole systems learning, idealism and activism, globalism, and ecology.

I share most of these qualities and considered myself a Core Cultural Creative. I also felt that people who fit into this group would be attracted to causes consistent with my theories about community development in that one-mile radius. This was the likely pool of buyers for the urban homes and lifestyle that I was promoting, and I continued studying them. It seemed that the musicians and writers on Music Row, the academics from the nearby universities, and the artistic types that I was serving fit the bill. In Ray's book, I learned that Cultural Creatives include people of all races, ages, and classes, and that the author felt that this subculture could have enormous social and political clout, if only it had awareness of itself as a cohesive unit.

Ray's book led to the discovery and evolution of LOHAS—Lifestyles of Health and Sustainability—and the LOHAS marketplace. It is the Cultural Creative subculture that started the LOHAS movement, and Ray suggested that the ranks were swelling 1 percent each year. LOHAS is not a specific category of products or services but rather a self-sufficient, ecologically friendly philosophy shared by a disparate set of businesses. They do this not only because it is the right thing to do but also because it is a more lucrative path. Natural and organic foods make up a large portion of the LOHAS market. Socially responsible investing is another emerging category, with Calvert Fund, Domini, and Renewal. I felt that the revitalization of the urban market related to LOHAS and that there was a good business case to be made for my work.

Through this kind of exploration, my sense of myself, and in turn my business, was evolving. Being creative and inventive was key to business success in the twenty-first century, and I was always looking for new methods and ideas as I was honing my trade and my ideas of community and urban neighborhoods.

But in these early days, my name was my brand and my customer base a source of the best referrals. I started inviting these good people to an annual cookout, which I hosted in Sevier Park, and asked them to bring a guest who might have real estate needs. I called it the "I Dealt with Deutschmann" party and sent written invitations. Miriam Myers, my designer of quirky campaigns, created an artistic T-shirt each year with an eclectic photograph of some neighborhood and an understated mention of my brand. I gave them to all in attendance. Some people later told me that they'd amassed the entire collection. I wonder if anyone could produce one today.

This is how my involvement in Nashville's core began and how some of my ideas were formed. The return to cities, and to the core, is happening across the globe. What we are experiencing in Nashville is not isolated, and one would hope that we can share best practices with many evolving urban centers and that we can serve as a great example. In the 2014 fall meeting of the Urban Land Institute (ULI), real estate developer Rob Speyer said that the urban migration is the biggest development opportunity in history and that cities are getting younger, greener, denser, more accessible, and more diverse and are teeming with energy and fun. He cited the estimate of 2.5 billion people moving to cities between now and 2050 and that cities are more important than ever in bringing people together. People come to cities because they crave real community, real networking with real people who have real faces—not a social network, not a virtual community. "It's the same reason people have been coming to cities since Damascus," he said, "and it is not being replaced by technology." He closed with a statement: "Cities are not just surviving, cities are thriving. Are you ready?"

Chapter 2

The Pattern That Connects

Somewhere there's a pattern
that connects, a tightly woven
mesh too fine to see.

—Dave Johnson

THIS SHORT LYRIC about the "pattern that connects" from my college roommate's song, written decades ago, means more and more to me as I get older. Life's experiences shape the pattern of who we are, and we use this pattern of experience to create what's to come. Certainly my own myriad of experiences created a pattern, shaping who I am and bringing me to the community building I do in Nashville. Even as a kid I was learning that community means more than going with the status quo; it often means thinking outside the box, playing the maverick. It can call for leadership, commitment, and a willingness to be open to all of life's lessons. I have learned this many times in my life as a preacher's kid, a hitchhiker, and a real estate practitioner. It keeps coming around. Like a person, communities are shaped by life experiences, influenced and shaped by those who are engaged.

My father, William Markert Deutschmann, was a Lutheran minister in Freemont, Ohio. My mother, Suzanne Graetz Deutschmann, was a school bus driver and a preacher's wife. She taught us how to be preacher's kids. When I was two years old, we moved to Boca Raton, Florida, and lived in the parsonage of Advent Lutheran Church. When I was nine, we moved to Alexandria, Virginia, and my father took a job as the director of American Missions for the Lutheran Church. Three years later, we moved to Columbia, Maryland.

You've probably heard a story or two about preachers' kids. We are notorious for being troublemakers. I think the premise is that we have to show our peers we aren't a "goody two-shoes." My sister, Maggie, my brother, Richard, and I were no different. My mother's brother, Robert Sylvester Graetz, was also an urban Lutheran minister, so to compound the situation, we had seven cousins who helped us further our rebellious ways.

My uncle's first congregation was in Montgomery, Alabama, where he worked alongside Martin Luther King and other civil rights leaders to lead the Montgomery bus boycott in 1955–1956. Known as that "white preacher from Montgomery," my uncle took his next calls to urban Los Angeles and then to Washington, D.C. My cousins had acquired a lot of urban experience growing up on the streets and were excellent role models for the Deutschmann brood of preacher's kids, which is to say that they were a little wild and packed with street smarts. We learned how to get into a fair bit of trouble with them.

Uncle Bob and his wife, Aunt Jeannie, were powerful influences in my life. When Uncle Bob accepted the call to be a minister in Montgomery, his family of four were the only white members of the 150-member congregation. There was a lot going on in Montgomery at the time. One night, he recalls, he got a call from one of his Sunday school teachers, Rosa Parks, who said, "Pastor, I did not give up my seat on the bus today." Uncle Bob, who was sympathetic to the civil rights action that was brewing, supported her, and one thing led to another. That's how Uncle Bob and Aunt Jeannie became leaders in the famous bus boycott, in which blacks decided that they would wreak economic havoc by staying off the bus. Bob and Jeannie soon joined other active civil rights leaders, including Martin Luther King Jr., E. D. Nixon, and Ralph Abernathy, and the rest, of course, is history. Bob's book, *A White Preacher's Memoir: The Montgomery Bus Boycott,* tells the story of my uncle's experience.

My Uncle Bob, Robert Graetz, with Martin Luther King, Jr.

The work that my aunt and uncle did in those historic times, and with those amazing leaders, had a strong influence on the work I would later do in Nashville. It taught me that change is possible, that those run-down houses along the city's center belong to hardworking people who deserve vitality in their neighborhoods, and that as a community we could do something about it. It taught me to more easily see those who might feel unseen. Uncle Bob also opened me up to being with people from different paths, which would later help me relate to almost anyone I met in the real estate business. And while I maintained a healthy skepticism of organized religion, I was interested in spiritual growth and connected communities and was always thirsty for a good dose of rebellion.

Perhaps my interest in real estate development began when my family moved to the planned city of Columbia, Maryland, in 1971. My family arrived in Columbia when Wilde Lake, one of the first of the city's ten self-contained villages, was taking shape. Each village was made up of a few connected neighborhoods with a central shopping center and centrally located schools. All neighborhoods and their community centers were connected by greenways and biking and walking trails. This is a model that Nashville, with its greenways, strives toward today.

My parents were attracted to Columbia because of the strong community. We went to church at the Interfaith Center, which housed a number of different faiths and denominations under the same roof. The Lutheran church that we attended shared times and services with other faiths. The center worked to promote shared values instead of focusing on differences. I believe that the strong community was influenced by aspects of "placemaking"—walkability and connectivity, design and form, all qualities we are aware of as we recreate urban neighborhoods in Nashville.

The city, conceived and founded by James Rouse, was fairly young at the time. Rouse was a developer who transformed the core in many cities from desolate to vibrant. He was responsible not only for Columbia's smaller, walkable neighborhood design but also for Harborplace in Baltimore and Faneuil Hall in Boston.

Rouse was a community builder. He designed the community based on human values, with the intent to not only shift away from the standard subdivision design but also to eliminate racial, social, and class segregation.

When Rouse conceived of Columbia in the 1960s, he set up dummy corporations to purchase land secretly so as not to drive up values. By doing this, he accumulated 10 percent of Howard County, just over fourteen thousand acres. There he set up what he envisioned would be a hundred-thousand-person community. This urban planning process became renowned and was led by the Work Group, a fourteen-member group of nationally recognized experts in the social sciences. They sought innovations in education, recreation, religion, and health care and looked for ways to enhance social interactions. Columbia's open classrooms, the Interfaith Center, and the health maintenance organization (HMO) came from these planning meetings.

I certainly enjoyed my first taste of entrepreneurialism in Columbia. Like so many entrepreneurs that I know today, I had a paper route for a few years, delivering the *Washington Post* every morning from 5 to 6 a.m., rain or shine. I first focused on my route, and with door knocking and "cold calls" doubled my business. But 110 papers were about the most I could reasonably deliver on a morning jaunt before school. So Whitey Hoover, my sales manager, who respected my initiative, gave me permission to sell subscriptions in other emerging neighborhoods. Columbia was growing like crazy, I had a good product, and for me it was an easy sale. I'd ride my bike to different neighborhoods, knocking on doors on Saturdays and early evenings, and sold a bunch. I became one of the top sales agents in the entire *Washington Post* region, won a bunch of free trips and prizes, and was initiated into sales. This was good preparation for my real estate career in Nashville, where, like in those early entrepreneurial days, I knocked on doors, soliciting and selling my real estate business.

In the summer after tenth grade, my family and two other families, including another Lutheran pastor—our minister at the Interfaith Center—got together for a couple of weeks of retreat and vacation at Deep Creek Lake in western Maryland. The other families, including the Lueckes, had kids our age. Mike was my best friend, and our parents had grown close. One night, when we came in from watching the stars, our folks asked us if we'd all like to move in together. The adults were thinking about living collectively, and we were all for it. Over the next year, our families got together and discussed the possibilities and pitfalls, filling large Post-it notes with their vision, hopes, and dreams. That next year, we found a sixteen-bedroom Civil War-era home just outside of Columbia on fourteen acres, the Homewood House, and each family sold their house and moved in.

Living at Homewood House was a life-changing experience for me. Our land was surrounded by thousands of acres of horse farms and fields, and we had a river at the edge of our property. There was an eight-stall horse barn. The Luecke girls got a horse,

The Homewood House in Ellicott City, Maryland.

Community meeting at the Homewood House.

and we arranged to board horses for others. We practiced collective living, dividing up tasks and chores and figuring out how to create a home with sixteen people including kids and teens. We had big chore charts, and everyone had to participate. I generally signed up to work outside, mowing the pastures and working in our big garden, but I also liked to make the big grocery shopping trips. Everyone of "adult" age, fourteen of us, had to sign up to cook one dinner, two people per dinner, for everyone once a week. Dinners were a big deal, and we all came together, sometimes in song and dance and celebration.

For the adults, it was supposed to be a place for nurturing the spirit, yet with five teens and preteens in the early mix, all preachers' kids, who grew into full-blown teens as the years passed, we ruled the roost. And, to the chagrin of the adults, I discovered the elder Luecke girl, Sue, and we became high school sweethearts. It was a big house, with lots of room for parties, and we took advantage, occasionally having hundreds of unruly guests at the house or down at the barn with a big bonfire. I'm sure my parents and the Luecke folks had some fine memories, but they probably shake their heads at some of what transpired.

At sixteen, I was beginning to struggle with authority, particularly with my father, and took a summer job for Christian Renewal Underway in a Sailing Experience (CRUISE). I moved to Miami, living in a room above a church in a seedy section of town, and worked for the summer as the second mate on a schooner taking youth groups from other churches to the Bahamas on seven- to nine-day journeys. I'd clean and stock the boat, help with the orientation, and when on the water help with all aspects of life on a sailboat. I remember how much Conrad, who ran the program that my dad had helped create, and others admired my father, but I, the preacher's kid, was out to find my own identity and to think about what religion and spirit meant to me. Typical teenager, very typical preacher's kid. It was a dream job, and it gave me a chance to sort some things out and to mature.

Back home again, I remember a lot of sessions in the "I'm OK, you're OK" era where we had to talk our truths and did a lot of group process. We learned to listen and to speak our truth even when we disagreed. Life at Homewood was a community-building experience, and we all worked hard to understand and work with our unique collection of synergies and personalities. This is not unlike the multitude of community meetings that shape our policy and plans in Nashville. Though we enjoyed the refuge of our home at the edge of the city, most of our work, school, and activities still centered around Columbia.

All of the teens attended Columbia schools, and eventually we all attended Wilde Lake High School. Mirroring the early evolution of Columbia, Wilde Lake was an experimental school. It worked with a system based on the Learning Activity Package (LAP). Students were not required to attend set classes and were allowed to advance their work with the LAPs at their own pace. I enjoyed the freedom in the system. Though I'd sometimes stay and play baseball and soccer outside, or enjoy a game of bridge with my friends in the common area, I also liked to pick one course and jam for hours.

I think this model was supposed to be a preparation for college and for life, where one has to take responsibility and be disciplined to create structure. But many teenagers were not able to manage themselves, and the majority did not "pass" in those first few years. Gradually, the teachers had to tighten down the system, and privileges were reserved for those who performed.

More than forty-five years after Columbia's founding, *Money* magazine and other publications now consistently rank the city as one of the best places to live in the United States. Columbia is still working to adapt to the times, and now it is looking at how to revitalize the downtown area, around Columbia Mall and Lake Kittamaqundi, where my brother Richard and his wife live today. The Downtown Columbia Plan was adopted in 2010. The plan describes adding density, with thirteen million square feet of additional retail, commercial, residential, hotel, and cultural development in the works and improvements in what is called the multi-nodal transportation system. This indicates that community development must constantly be renewed to better serve the people and the times.

Though I am now more attracted to older cities in our country and the world, I do think that living in Rouse's Columbia, combined with life at the Homewood House, has had a huge impact on my community work today. The village concept, with all of the necessary services, is something we seek to recreate in our neighborhood commercial districts and on our corridors. Columbia's built-in greenway system, which penetrates deeply into all of its neighborhoods, is something we are trying to emulate. And my experience both with Columbia and the Homewood House, intentional communities, reminds me that we can plan and design for best outcomes.

Columbia was designed for walkability, bikability, and connection by public transportation. Nashville is making some good strides with its greenway system but needs to continue to penetrate deeply into all urban neighborhoods. And we are still struggling to implement a viable long-term public transportation system that connects the dots. This is now one of the foremost concerns for Mayor Megan Barry, who won a historic election in 2015, becoming the first woman to lead our city.

When I finished at Wilde Lake, I decided to forgo college and set out hitchhiking. I may have been following my older sister Maggie's path. At sixteen, she had moved out to her own commune and at seventeen hitched out to South Dakota to work with the Wounded Knee Defense Committee, supporting those who had been arrested in protests for the rights of the Sioux tribe and other indigenous people.

Mayor Megan Barry at a Village sales meeting, talking about social justice.

I learned quickly that the road is an adventure and that every ride can change your life. I hitchhiked more than twenty thousand miles during these years, in the United States, Canada, South America, and Europe. This was the mid-1970s, when hitchhiking was pretty mainstream and safe. It was a life-changing experience, and I met a host of extremely interesting people. The roads are endless, and your journey can change with every ride. It was one of the best educations I could have asked for—one that prepared me for sales and entrepreneurship. Why? Because when you know how to engage myriad types of people, when you know how to get onto their wavelength and speak their language, you can catch their vision and provide them with exactly what they need. It also taught me how to rely on my own resources, imperative for anyone starting out.

Each time a car slowed to a stop for me, I had a chance to engage with a driver in a new way, intuiting what kind of person was now my host and sharing with him who I wanted to be at that moment. I hitchhiked through the fall, and by October I was on the frigid plains in Minnesota. Hitchhiking this northern route across the country, as the days were growing darker and cooler, was not a great idea. With the shortening days, it was easy to get stuck without a ride, and I had to tuck in under a bridge or in a field, using wits and resources to keep from freezing.

Fortunately, a recently divorced man from New York City picked me up as he drove his trailer across the country "to clear his head." We were both on an adventure and hit it off. As it goes, we were both reading Carlos Castanada books on shamanism, including his book *The Teachings of Don Juan*, and we talked for hours about the practice of conscious dreaming, a practice of the shamans in ancient Mexico. Kindred spirits on the road. We traveled the Badlands and into Yellowstone. I drove with him for about two weeks before he dropped me off in Utah. He had gotten me out of the cold and a long way on my journey.

On that first hitchhiking adventure, I wanted to make it across the country on a hundred dollars. When I set foot in Berkeley, California, I still had fifty dollars in my pocket. It was a good lesson in ingenuity and the kindness of people who took me in. As long as I was a good passenger, the world provided me good rides.

I moved in with my sister in Berkeley, and one of our housemates was Jeff Raz, an artist and a performing juggler. He was involved with a troupe called the Pickle Family Circus and had a performance that included balls, clubs, torches, balance, and vaudeville. The juggling fascinated me, and while I was to be in town for just three months, I decided to learn the art and take it on the road.

Later, when I hitchhiked out of Berkeley, I passed away idle hours practicing the art while waiting for rides. As I added new tricks and showcased them for passing traffic, I found that this new skill set helped me get rides. I was learning the value of showmanship.

Over the years, I would expand my juggling skills, first learning three and four balls, then clubs, then passing clubs to do intricate juggling patterns with partners. My daughter, Chelsea Kyle Gifford, was often a prop, and she smiled and laughed when I performed with her, throwing her high in the air when she was a baby, standing on my hands when she was learning to walk, and working with her as she got older and bigger, standing her on my shoulders. She was a crowd-pleaser and definitely attracted customers.

I even learned other skills fit for the stage, such as group passing routines, devil sticks, swinging clubs, fire eating, and even clowning. I also tried busking, which is the term for street performance and passing the hat. Though I never really liked asking for money for myself, I did it from time to time, as it is a good gauge of entertainment value. If you are entertaining, the hat fills; if not, it remains empty.

I wasn't just a juggler—or malabarista, as they say down south—eventually juggling clubs, machetes, bowling balls, fire, and whatever else was at hand. I would also become a juggler of roles, interests, plans, and endeavors. My wife, my friends, and my executive teams would come to know me as someone who could track a number of things, much like a juggler tracks the flight of an object in an intricate pattern. Sales, business creation, and community building all require a degree of showmanship—an engagement that gauges interest and value in a product or experience—and juggling became a metaphor for me in my work.

We almost never know what we are building once we start, but if we go in the direction of what feels good, what interests and challenges us, even something as seemingly benign as juggling can hand us incredible opportunities.

My juggling became somewhat reckless as I moved into my early adulthood. For example, in grad school at Thunderbird, I put together a routine for the school talent show called "Danger Man." I juggled to a David Bromberg song of the same name. The lyrics are: "I'm a danger man, from a dangerous city, and I lead a dangerous life; I have a dangerous car that goes dangerous speeds and a very hazardous wife. I have sixteen or seventeen dangerous girlfriends, not counting one or two. Look out kid, you don't want to get hit, 'cause I'm dangerous to you. You'd better look out."

I had choreographed a routine with an entourage of flappers and gangsters who brought in my props, and I juggled knives, wine bottles, machine guns, and fire on the stage. We took first place. This song mirrored my attitude toward risk and reward. I was a risk taker, had lived on the edge for many years, and was now looking to shift risk/reward for community good. And, after a nomadic period in life, I was ready for some grounding.

My parents, when I was in college, had invested in a company in Minneapolis called "Come to Your Senses," which sold household products like bath soaps and salts, incense, and things that might enhance adult relationships. My father worked a lot in Minneapolis, the headquarters of the American Lutheran Church, and in his travels he met Dan Weiss. One of the products that the store sold was futons, and they sold so well that Dan decided to launch a manufacturing company called "Sun Tui," which means "the joyous / the gentle" in Japanese. He was raising $100,000 to start the enterprise and invited my folks, my brother, and me to participate. I invested $5,000, got a 5 percent stake, and took a seat on the board, representing the family holdings.

The company grew rapidly, eventually reaching $10 million in gross revenue, and for a time was very profitable, with net income approaching $1 million per year. Regular distributions became a helpful part of my income stream as I worked to find my place. I enjoyed being part of a board, traveling to Minneapolis to tour the factory and to support company growth. I was a novice at business and probably did not have much to offer, but Dan took me under his wing. Growth accelerated when we got a contract with Pier 1, selling futons to all of their outlets. We decided to diversify, getting into the business of manufacturing frames, and expanded the factory.

One of the things that I learned in hindsight is that a company in growth mode has to watch its capital. Sun Tui relied on bank financing, never launching a second round of investor financing. The new frame division in particular was complex and capital intensive. Margins started to fall and cash flow weakened. Sales, however, were strong and we landed new contracts with Sam's Club and other large outlets. But a series of events and decisions threw the company into a spin. The company computer and inventory system had glitches and crashed. The plant had a fire, which shut down production.

It was amazing how fast a company could fall apart with a couple of poor decisions and some bad luck. The leadership team decided that we had to sell the business and sought and found a suitor. However, in the process, while waiting for the deal to close, the company was "factoring receivables," meaning that it was borrowing against incoming orders. When in the late '80s the deal to sell fell through, the company was overleveraged and collapsed. It was a painful lesson that I have not forgotten, particularly later when I made defensive moves in preparation for the Great Recession.

I moved to Nashville in 1985 with some juggling skill in tow, degrees in zoology and Spanish, an MBA in international management, and enough income at that time from the futon company dividends to supplement my income. I perceived myself as jack-of-all-trades, master of none, but had come to a place where I was ready to settle down.

I was ambitious and wanted to do something with my new international degree, so I started a company called the Spherical Exchange, alluding to the juggling as metaphor. I reached out to people whom I'd met in my South American travels and started importing artisan goods. The business backfired when some clothing I had purchased was impounded. The content, which I had been led to believe was a cotton/wool blend, actually had some acrylic in the weave. The product and I were investigated until finally, months later, I was instructed go to the Nashville airport, to a loading dock where they store impounded product, to remove and relabel hundreds of scarves. That venture not working out, I kept searching for a career.

I took a job as a window washer with a firm called Transparency Works, run by a spirit-filled man named Venu. For Venu, washing windows was part of his spiritual practice, and he demanded excellence. I discovered that washing windows was therapeutic and felt like a personal cleansing.

Over the years—and something that continues today—I'd been inspired to seek spiritual practice, and had, as a reformed preacher's kid, a tolerant and expansive spiritual worldview. I became interested in an art teacher at the University of Maryland, a Sioux Indian elder my friends and I had met because he lived down the road from the Homewood House. We helped him prepare for the traditional sweat lodges, which he led with chants and prayers to Father Earth and Mother Sky. We also helped him prepare his land and observed from a distance when other Sioux elders came for vision quests. This practice deepened my appreciation for nature and ritual and allowed me an opportunity to view another's beliefs and the importance of tolerance when building community.

I'd also been attracted to a group that studied the teaching of Gurdjieff, a Russian philosopher. We practiced the ways of this teacher and of his disciple Ouspensky, who wrote the book *The Fourth Way,* which holds that a person is a collection of individuals—each of whom has a unique personality. The goal of this practice is to gain awareness such that this collection of individuals becomes one, helping you get more control over your life with the possibility to become enlightened. I still reflect on this practice today. It has helped me to focus on the many pieces of my agenda for our community.

One practice, Alaya, was particularly appealing to me. Created by my friends Reta Lawler and Thomas Huffman, both trained therapists, Alaya is an integrated practice of mind, body, and soul. It combines a variety of disciplines, including meditation, music, and traditional therapy. My new friends in my budding Nashville community signed up for an intensive group process, a nine-month Alaya practice. The work demanded that I take a deep look at myself, my core being, and what moves me in this world and life. Everyone, we were taught, has a key emotional trait they carry through life. I discovered that one of my key traits is feeling that I'm not good enough. My mother reminded me that I was a middle child and got no attention—perhaps this is why I sought to prove myself in my community. It is important for me, even today, to keep this in perspective in my work and to therefore give myself some grace when seeking to accomplish lofty life goals. The Alaya practice taught me self-worth and valuable communication tools, like active listening and empathy, that serve me in both my business and community work. I also did inner work, mourning the death of my father. I worked to find my role in my new community, as Nashville was becoming home.

I had gotten a real estate license almost as soon as I arrived but had left it dormant. When I truly decided to pursue real estate, I firmly committed myself to a minimum of seven years. I was determined to pursue a career with value, something where I could create work with meaning. I started selling homes. Now working with Renaissance, I put out a newsletter in the Hillsboro Village neighborhoods letting my constituency know that "A Renaissance Is Coming," showcasing my first couple of home listings. With entrepreneurial spirit, I knocked on doors and talked to people about opportunities in the neighborhood. One customer, Joe Rogers, worked for the *Tennessean* and had written an article in the early 1990s about how difficult it was to buy a home. Years later, Joe reminded me that I saw the article, called him, and told him that I could get him into a home, which I did, giving him a futon as a housewarming gift.

In many ways, I got my start in real estate with the *Nashville Scene,* which ran a regular feature called "Hot Homes," written by Bernie Sheahan from 1989 to 1995. I was an early advertiser, listed quirky homes in a character neighborhood, and had a lot of homes in the column. I remember working with Bernie when I was selling a home at the top of Cedar Lane, "Castle Corner," for Randy Rayburn. The home had, I counted, eighty-eight windows and a room below with a separate stairwell for "the help," all notably featured in the article. Bernie ran the article, the house sold to another wonderful urban pioneer, and Randy used the money from the sale to fund his restaurant Sunset Grill in Hillsboro Village, a great investment and an institution for many years.

My real estate practice grew in a stair-step manner. I sold twenty-eight homes in each of the first couple of years, then forty-three homes for a couple of years, then sixty-two for a couple, and then jumped into the eighties. With each jump, I added tools and talent to my evolving team and enjoyed bringing creativity and spirit to my practice. When Kelly Coty approached me with a business called Prix de Solde, with something she called "home staging," I was all ears. It was often difficult to convince a seller to make the adequate changes to get a home sold, a process that was often fraught with emotion. Kelly proposed a concept that transformed the listing process. She gave me a free trial on a "little old lady" listing, which I'd had on the market for months without an offer. The home was cluttered with years of living, and the seller was unable, physically or with the proper vision, to get the house into "sales" shape. Kelly worked her magic, and the home sold in a week. I added a new twist to my trade, and home staging came to Nashville.

My early real estate practice coincided with my search for meaning, and I was regularly visiting and attending workshops at Hollyhock.

One in particular was aptly named "Spirit and Business," which was a precursor to a later workshop, in partnership with the Social Venture Network, called the Social Venture Institute (SVI), which continues to this day. Spirit and Business spoke to me; I was searching for spirit and meaning, and I was learning how to translate that into a real estate business. These were my formative years in the business and influenced my thinking when I later started Village Real Estate.

During that time, newly elected Bill Clinton spoke to the Social Venture Network (SVN), a group that I was involved with, in Washington, D.C. His aspirations and vision inspired me in the work that I was doing, and I was honored to have a chance to meet him. I stood in the queue with none other than the Western-born yogi and spiritual teacher Ram Dass, who was connected with some of the leaders at SVN. I had read his books, including *Be Here Now,* and had a fascinating conversation with him as we slowly made our way forward. As we approached the stage, I reached out to meet the president, but as he shook my hand he saw my companion and enthusiastically said "Ram Dass" and proceeded to have a conversation with him, still holding my hand. I waited patiently, a little awestruck, until they finished, and the president finally greeted me and released me from the extended shake.

Chelsea on her 2016 South American adventure.

Fast-forward to 2016, and my daughter, Chelsea, who works in outdoor therapy for troubled teens, was at a retreat in Maui, Hawaii. One of her fellow leaders from a program she worked with in Colorado had moved on and now worked as an assistant to

Ram Dass, and Chelsea was invited to stay at his home. Chelsea and Ram Dass hit it off, and she shared with him the story of when he met her dad. He has a keen mind and quite the sense of humor, and he was tickled to share that connection with my daughter. This is just another small example of the pattern that connects, bringing all life experience to bear.

As we age, we shift a few degrees, but the search for meaning continues. Also in 2016, through the Entrepreneurs' Organization, a group that I'm involved with, I attended a session at Sewanee called "Monk on the Mountain." There, I listened and learned from Dandapani, a former Hindu monk who now teaches practice to entrepreneurs. Dandapani considers the brain a tool. He spoke of awareness and the mind, describing awareness as the light that shines in the brain, illuminating where it sends its beam, creating consciousness in that area of the mind. Using willpower, you can move awareness and focus with intention, something that we can practice. Without willpower, awareness goes where it will, and one creates a practice in distraction. Dandapani called the practice "Unwavering Focus." What a great lesson for entrepreneurs, who are prone to distraction! He asked us to define our practice, and I described mine at that time as a practice of compassion. Phil Ryan, my friend and colleague, had given me a book that I'd been studying, *Training in Compassion,* by Norman Fischer. I'd been meditating on these Zen teachings for some time, so it was wonderful to have the opportunity to discuss and share this work with a well-trained practitioner.

Dave Johnson and Mark juggling in Arcata, California.

All of my experiences, from our community living at the Homewood House to hitchhiking to juggling to spiritual seeking, were navigation points in my life. Like the compass rose in the corner of a map, they guided me in the right direction. They gave me many opportunities to see from another's point of view and to recognize the importance of tolerance and appreciation when building community. They were pieces of the pattern, the pattern that connects.

I am reminded that Dave Johnson, my college roommate who penned "The Pattern That Connects," was also an accomplished juggler. We were juggling in the Arcata town square one day when Jeff Jacobsen approached. Jeff was also a juggler, and we passed some clubs. Later, when I interviewed for the job working with the killer whales, Jeff realized that we had that juggling connection, and of course I got the job. And because I got that job, and then because my boat caught on fire, I ended up in Nashville. Ah, the pattern that connects!

Chapter 3

Evolution of the One-Mile Radius

We do not go to work only to earn an income but to find meaning in our lives. What we do is a large part of what we are.

—Alan Ryan

IN THOSE EARLY days in my career, for reasons you've now learned, I was known as the "Juggling Realtor." I hung my real estate license first with the Gene Lynch Company, and I wore Converse sneakers and suspenders, even when showing houses. My early *Nashville Scene* ads often featured juggling photographs, and I sometimes juggled at my open houses to attract business. I even wore the suspenders and juggling attire to

Greater Nashville Realtors (GNR) award events instead of the formal attire that was the norm in the Realtor community. Indeed, early in my involvement with the GNR, at a Metro Council roast, I was asked to roast my councilman, Mansfield Douglas, and did the job somewhat literally, and likely in poor taste here in the South, by juggling fire clubs and reaching around his body such that he was between me and the flame. I was learning how to stand out in a crowd, but I was hungry for something more.

As I was practicing real estate in Nashville, I had been strengthening my ties to Hollyhock, the retreat center on Cortes Island in British Columbia, where I first learned about socially responsible business. I was even more active in the Social Venture Network (SVN) through my friendship with Joel, who was a founding member. This was a group of more than four hundred business owners, mostly with incomes of $5 million gross and upward, who were committed to a "just and sustainable economy." This was a group of profitable enterprises, not for profit, or "social" enterprises, and politicos, exploring what were at the time a unique set of leadership skills. SVN members included Ben Cohen of Ben and Jerry's, Gary Hirshberg of Stonyfield Yogurt, Drummond Pike of the Tides Foundation, Gregor Robertson (now the mayor of Vancouver) of Happy Planet Juice Company, and Anita Roddick of The Body Shop. Each had their way of using business for social change, and I'd been contemplating how I could do the same.

In the early 1990s, Hollyhock hosted a series of workshops, titled Body and Soul, on the West Coast, and my juggling dovetailed with my business world. Partnered with *New Age Journal,* Hollyhock brought in celebrity authors, and I was invited to use juggling to introduce the speakers. I was called a Weaver and wove into my message juggling metaphors related to the work of the authors. I've used the method to drive points home in many speaking engagements over the years. Juggling, when coupled with speaking, is extremely effective. People remember the images; they remember your words.

Gregor Robertson, Joel Solomon, and Mark on Cortes Island.

A Hollyhock weekend workshop with celebrity authors could attract more than two thousand participants in conferences that we held in Portland, Seattle, and San Francisco. I introduced Wayne Dyer, an author of over forty self-help and spiritual books, whose lecture that day had to do with the "seven principles." I used all of my balls that day, working up to seven to make the point. I introduced David Whyte, author and poet, who was delighted and surprised when I juggled his introduction. I especially enjoyed working with and introducing Jon Kabat-Zinn, who was then touting his book *Wherever You Go, There You Are*. Years later, my longtime managing broker Bobbie Noreen still uses this phrase when an agent exits the company.

Hollyhock then offered me the privilege of introducing Julia Cameron, author of *The Artist's Way*. Wanting to be a good host, I first read her book. She recommended, among other things, practicing something called "morning pages," where you write in a journal for ten minutes each day to unlock creativity and to let your spirit soar.

I began doing my morning pages, and on the first day I wrote about my career path, real estate. In my musings about "what I should do with my life," I noted that I was good at selling real estate, that it would be a shame to abandon what I'd started, and that the real estate business could benefit from a social impact model. Furthermore, I had a vision for neighborhoods and cities, and I wanted to have a role in building my community. I had that "aha!" moment and realized that, if I wanted to achieve these goals, I needed to start a real estate company. As it turns out, I never did meet Julia Cameron at the Hollyhock/*New Age* event that year; she took ill and missed the conference. If she ever reads this, though, I'd like her to know how much she influenced me with her work.

Mark standing in front of original home of Village Real Estate.

It took eight months, a lot of phone calls, paperwork, and sleepless nights after that initial "aha!" moment, but on October 6, 1996, we finally did it: Village Real Estate Services was born. Our first office was in the upstairs of a very sweet converted old stone bungalow at 1910 Twenty-First Avenue South, in Hillsboro Village. There were just a few of us—two agents, Scott Troxel and Karen Hoff; an administrative

ORIGINAL MISSION STATEMENT

VILLAGE PEOPLE, L.L.C.

To form a holding company of philosophically aligned business ventures and investments. This company will bring together a pool of resources, both human and material, that will support the well being of successful, progressive, urban neighborhoods, and related business ventures that in one way or another support healthier lifestyles and culture that is sustainable, ecologically sound, and builds long term community, with the potential of paying a steady return to investors.

In order to enhance the investment, and to show his dedication to the new venture, Mark Deutschmann will be rolling in his ownership interests in of Willma I. Solomon Village Limited (Willma Partnership), The Wilber Partnership (Wilber Partnership), DJB Enterprises, L.L.C. (DJB Enterprises), 1221 Partners, L.L.C. (1221 Partners), as well as his ownership of 1016 Caruthers Avenue. Each of these ventures will be described below. The primary purpose of creating this holding company is to launch Village Real Estate Services, which offers sales and service to neighborhood commercial and urban residential districts.

Mark showing off the new company logo.

team of two; and myself—but we set out to change the way real estate is practiced. One of our first slogans, mirroring my search for self, was "Find Your Place."

I formed a limited liability corporation under the name of Village People, LLC (perhaps a reflection of the diversity in our organization today), set forth a mission statement, and closed with a round of investment capital from friends and family. A good portion of my angel funding came from friends I'd met at SVN and Hollyhock. Many of my cohorts from SVN invested in my vision. As part of our offering and key to the mission of the organization, I put 5 percent of the company into our nonprofit, the Village Fund. I had structured the deal such that I put up virtually all of value that I owned. My rental properties, shares of local companies that I owned, and even my house were put into the new company. And there was a deal that favored shareholders; I took a low equity stake, with the promise that if I performed and paid back shareholder within a fixed time, the shares would flip so that I had the majority. The faster the money returned, the more I would get. But I also put all of my sales income into the company, was confident in my sales ability, and was motivated by the vision.

The idea was to attract agents who had a sense of social mission, sell a lot of homes, revitalize our neighborhood commercial districts, and use the Village Fund to support important causes existing in our community. I hoped to gain buy-in from agents, staff, and vendor partners and then gain support and buy-in from our customers. Our immediate goal was to service the real estate needs in our midtown communities, including Hillsboro Village, Germantown, East Nashville, Sylvan Park, and 12South. We then planned to move downtown, as we believed our city was ripe for new urban neighborhoods. In essence, we focused on transitioning neighborhoods that had been affected by urban flight and on introducing Nashville to this next iteration of older neighborhoods—using versions of my one-mile radius concept to help Nashville create a solid residential core.

At that time, Joel had moved back to Vancouver to work with Carol Newell at the Renewal Partners and Endswell Foundation. Carol, a remarkable woman who had inherited millions, had made a decision to spend down her assets in British Columbia, using Renewal and Endswell as a vehicle for social change. She put $14 million into Endswell, which was used to support nonprofit and social-profit organizations, and another $20 million into Renewal Partners. Renewal was an investment vehicle, and investments were made based on social return. The premise was that this concentration of funds could make a difference in a community.

Joel was tapped to head both entities, and investments were made over the years, again with the intent to spend down the capital. Carol went on to found Play BIG, an organization that encourages those who have inherited over $25 million to "wake up" the sleeping capital and invest it in something that has meaning. Prior to his move, in the spirit of maintaining our partnership and with the thought to further our philosophies of money and of our independent interdependence, Joel and I traded 10 percent of the equity in our respective companies. So Joel was my largest shareholder at Village, and I gained a share in JSco, Joel's company, which was now investing with Renewal. For this I like to say affectionately that I got the title of "Director of Being Here" when I regularly visit Vancouver.

I was impressed by Joel's new work and also impressed by Judy Wicks, who had been an SVN leader in the late 1980s and early 1990s and the owner of a successful restaurant operation in Philadelphia called the White Dog Cafe. Judy was a proponent of something she termed the "local living economy." She began a discussion about how local businesses can provide great value to society. The community work we do, the employees we pay, and the charities we fund, when locally based, can have a profound impact. When it is all locally focused, the volunteer work, local salaries, and donations reverberate through a community. Compared to a large international company that often distributes profits around the country and the world, most local, home-based companies tend to leave a deeper impression on the community.

At SVN, many of the national and global companies had scaled up, sold, and lost some of their original mission when they were absorbed by larger multinational corporations. Events like these triggered conversations within SVN about successful exit strategies of a socially responsible organization and what a founder/owner might do to "be the tail that wags the dog." When Stonyfield later sold to Dannon, lessons had been learned, and the founder and CEO, Gary Hirshberg, negotiated an exit in a way that influences Dannon to this day. Some of Stonyfield's social business practices were espoused by Dannon, and the larger organization leveraged its network and distribution center to introduce the Stonyfield brand throughout Europe. Gary gives his account of this experience in his book *Stirring It Up*.

Judy went on, in 2001, to found the Business Alliance for Local Living Economies (BALLE, pronounced bolly), to nurture and curate the emergence of a new economy, one that supports the health and prosperity of all people and regenerates the vital ecosystems upon which our economy depends. She believes that with local ownership comes local accountability; when you live in the community where your business decisions are felt, you have the understanding to make better decisions. Likewise, the local impact within a one-mile radius espouses all of these attributes. She shares her stories in her book, *Good Morning, Beautiful Business: The Unexpected Journey of an Activist Entrepreneur and Local-Economy Pioneer.*

These stories and people influenced the creation of my company, and I was proud of the new business model I'd conceived for Village. At the time, in the late 1990s, we were well into the dot-com era, and I had seen companies ramp up from valuations of $0 to valuations of over $5 billion in short order. The Internet was allowing new ideas and new twists on old ideas to blossom to big audiences. Venture capital groups were funding these ideas and backing entrepreneurs with small companies, and many were going public to big cash infusions.

But what if Yahoo had given 5 percent to a Yahoo fund and the company had then gone to the $5 billion level? That fund would be worth $250 million now that Yahoo has just been sold. What if each of the new dot-com companies—eBay, Google, Facebook, etc.—had given some of their company away at inception, before their leap in value? This was my inspiration for the Village Fund. The ownership concept was not dependent on profitability, which can be manipulated. With ownership, ultimate value to the community is proportionate to the valuation of the company for its shareholders. Given that founder/owners work to create wealth for themselves and shareholders, an ownership model would protect the integrity of the Village Fund.

My aim with the Village Fund was to provide a boost to neighborhood nonprofits. With a little support, these local nonprofits would do much for their communities: providing needed assistance in various forms to low-income residents, creating beauty through art programs, enhancing walkability with parks and greenways, and providing educational support programs for parents and their children. In Nashville, there were many nonprofits doing community work that we wanted to support, and now we had a good tool for involvement and impact within that one-mile radius.

I gave the 5 percent of ownership to the Tides Foundation. I chose the Tides Foundation because of its commitment to social responsibility and because I knew the founder, Drummond Pike, from SVN. Village Fund distributions were to be donor advised, meaning that we made the gifting recommendations and then let Tides vet the nonprofits to ensure compliance. The plan was to give most of our money locally, to build relationships with many of the nonprofits, and to enhance monetary gifting with the volunteer efforts of our team. My early angel shareholders supported the concept. It was an ambitious plan for the two agents and two staff people who were with me when we launched.

Now the Village Fund receives 5 percent of all distributions to Village shareholders. Given that Village now includes a number of companies, including Core Development, the Village Fund has enjoyed increased returns. However, that is just a fraction of the money we give back. Much of the money now comes from our other stakeholders: our agents, our vendors, and our clients. Our sales agents are very generous, and one of the practices we advocate is a gifting per transaction. We ask our agents how much they want to pledge per transaction and then take that amount from their closings. And we ask our partners such as SWBC, a mortgage partner, and Rudy Title and Escrow, a closing partner, to give on a regular basis. Sometimes we even ask our customers to contribute.

When an agent lists a home for a client, he or she often creates a net sheet that shows customers what they will receive at a particular sales price when they close. The net sheet calculates the commissions, the closing costs, the title insurance, and any other incidental costs and shows customers their bottom line.

On my net sheets during those early days, I added the additional category of "contribution to the Village Fund," which I would leave blank. This gave me a chance to talk about the work of the fund and what we were doing in the community and to make a "pre-ask" to my customers for a donation. I'd ask them how much they would be willing to give if I got them top dollar for their home. Generally, this was something they would contemplate, and I would ask again as we negotiated a final contract. In a rising market it was easy, because customers were creating significant equity and were more than willing to add a contribution to the Village Fund at the closing.

We learned pretty quickly that one of the best things about the Village Fund was that it allowed us as agents to connect with our neighbors. Donations could be accompanied by action and engagement. An engaged agent was a community builder, and the community appreciated the action. That connection, and the fact that everyone needed housing and that people liked to work with people who supported their cause, created a virtuous cycle in which an agent can receive customers as a result of the connection.

In the early days, John Sherman, a Village shareholder, advised me on the fund. John, the former executive director of the Tennessee Environmental Council (TEC) and an environmental grant writer by profession, helped set forth the mission for our gifting. Village Fund gifts were smaller back then, so we focused on ways to align with our urban neighborhoods where we were practicing. We made the decision to exclude health-related initiatives, given that this is the focus of more than three hundred health care companies in our region. We decided to allow funding for a nonprofit's overhead, something that other funders, who focus on an organization's special projects, don't do.

The Village Fund also contributed to Hands On Nashville (HON), an organization that continues to do a lot of work for our public schools. In the early years of the fund, our group participated in a community day at Hume-Fogg High School, downtown on Broadway. Our growing team of Village agents joined others to repair a disheveled interior courtyard, painting the walls, weeding, gardening, painting furniture, and redecorating. Our efforts transformed the place. We did our work on a Saturday, when the students were out, and heard that the students were pleasantly shocked when they returned to the courtyard on Monday. How nice it must have felt to know that the community cared enough to put energy into an important space for the students. We have maintained a very deep relationship with HON through the years.

The Village Fund supported the Oasis Center's work with troubled teens. We were passionate about the cause and wanted to contribute our talents in addition to monetary funding. I organized a workshop for the sixty-two counselors and staff members and taught them how to juggle. We started by making our own juggling balls, as I had a method that used tennis balls, pellets, and funnels to create a perfectly weighted juggle ball that didn't bounce away when dropped. I then taught them how to juggle and how to teach others how to juggle. Nearly all of them were juggling at the end of the workshop. The goal was to bring juggling to the kids, because I knew the skill would promote self-confidence and discipline, traits that the Oasis Center was teaching. Over the years, I've heard from many of the folks as they've shared stories of how juggling gave them a unique and powerful way to help so many teens.

We gave back to the environment through causes such as Bring Urban Recycling to Nashville Today (BURNT), which at the time was trying to rid our city of the downtown incinerator that spewed unwanted pollutants into the air. It was located on what is now the West Cumberland Park, with our premier riverside attraction, the Ascend Amphitheater. Each donation was making a difference, and the impact was perceptible, as the work of the organizations effected change.

We also supported the Tennessee Environmental Council (TEC), which fights for clean air and water in our state, one of the first organizations to do so. The TEC hosts a yearly fundraiser called the Green Tie Affair. The event features both a silent and live auction, and we helped find the items to sell and participated in the auction as well. I auctioned myself, offering to "sell a home" at no commission, meaning that I would forgo my commission and sell the home at no cost to the seller. I always made sure that there were a few good prospects at the event so that the bidding would be lively. I would juggle for the crowd while the auction was happening, which was certainly good for drawing attention and usually resulted in the highest auction item pricing at the event. People knew it was a reliable investment and bid on me for a good cause.

This led to a deeper involvement, and I hosted both the event and the patrons party through the years. We pulled in celebrity musicians, including Kris Kristofferson, Rodney Crowell, and the Del Beatles, to play the TEC patrons party, which pleased the crowds and raised lots of money. Al and Tipper Gore were the hosts in 2001, just after Al had lost his presidential bid. I really enjoyed being the patron chair that year and found that our guests were gracious and that Al was very funny, which was surprising after he'd been portrayed as "stiff" in the media. Al was moving on from politics and was focused on climate change, having penned *Earth in the Balance* in the early 1990s. It was an honor to be a host, representing my company and the Village Fund, and I was proud of the connection with an early climate change champion.

To keep the momentum going within my community of agents and staff at Village, we have implemented urban real estate training for our agents. We are big on education, so we have a program called Village University, offering year-round training and seminars to help our agents become better stewards of the community. Our urban training now includes concepts such as smart growth, healthy urban in-fill, and affordable and attainable urban housing. We talk about the concept of urban density and why reuse of existing infrastructure is healthier than continued sprawl.

Village agents on the bus touring neighborhoods.

We even do bus tours, affectionately called "urban domination tours," given the ever-changing landscape, with our agents, allowing agent experts in each neighborhood to update the rest of us on what is happening.

Village University offers over two hundred training sessions per year. Some are in the form of vLabs, where a particular technology or real estate app is discussed. Some are hands-on sessions, in which an agent might do some "time blocking" or learn how to build a better database. Some deal with contracts and forms, others with prospecting and lead generation. Some are practical and provide immediate solutions; others are geared to help an agent become a lifelong professional.

We have a robust program called Village Collaborative, a yearlong boot camp that is available to all agents who come to the company and even to existing agents. If an agent joins a Club which leads to the Collaborative, they undergo a one-year boot camp full of practical training and required sales activity.

If agents complete Village Collaborative and have not doubled their sales production, we will not collect any company splits from their sales for the next year. It is a great promise, and we now require all new agents coming to the company to recruit. Our training is terrific, and we feel that we benefit even if agents don't double their production. Most do, and many have become extremely successful.

Our sales meeting, called 51 Minutes, is generally packed. Our training room can handle a maximum of about a hundred agents, so the meeting can spill out into the corridors. Our broker team leads the meetings, which we divide into small, interesting segments. "What Would You Do?" covers a real contract issue, and the agents are asked how they would handle the situation. This is often a rousing discussion, and the session is geared to allow agents to hear different perspectives. We talk about "Selling Nashville," and the agents have an opportunity to share their new listings. Our agents sell over 30 percent of our own company listings, and we often look for a match in which one agent's listing suits another agent's buying needs. We have another segment called "X Factor," where our experienced agents talk about the things they do that make them successful. We encourage our agents to have a unique selling proposition (USP), something that they do that no other agent does.

Bobbie Noreen speaking at 51 Minutes.

We also love to hear success stories, and we often conclude the meeting with "Happy Endings," in which three or four agents share a successful outcome to a sales or community situation. Every year we learn more from our training and our experience, and Nashville's communities benefit from it. We enrich each other's lives and make the community stronger. Together, we have achieved so much.

Throughout the years, I found that the more I developed and grew as a person, the more the Village Fund grew, a symbiotic relationship. The experiences that informed my work on the Village

Fund often came outside of my normal work hours, exploring parts of myself that real estate wasn't necessarily part of. As a former zoologist, trained in a marine concentration, I miss the water and often long to be near the ocean. To compensate, I took up river kayaking and paddling with friends and supporters of the Tennessee Scenic River Association on rivers in Tennessee and still enjoy an occasional adventure on the Ocoee.

Deep in the Grand Canyon after 9/11.

Mark in his kayak, nose-diving in a rapid.

The river experience is one of the best feelings in life: being in a boat, working with the river, looking for passage, knowing we are all stewards of the earth. It is a metaphor for life, I suppose. You navigate the rapids, choosing twists and turns that determine your destiny. It is important to be in the moment, to make sure you take a pure stroke, keep your balance, and try to keep your head out of the water. If you do go under, find your center, keep your cool, and roll up.

Because of this experience with kayaking, it became easier for me to maintain cool and calm when faced with business, family, and community hurdles. I can more readily find my center. I am more driven to take the kind of risks that have greater reward.

In 2001, I had a chance to go rafting down the Colorado River through the Grand Canyon. Drummond Pike, the founder of the Tides Foundation, is also a river guide, and he pulls together a select group each year for this sixteen-day journey. About twenty-five of us, including many friends of Hollyhock and SVN, were readying for the trip, coming from all parts of the country, and we were all prepared to gather in Flagstaff, Arizona, on September 18. My birthday is September 11, and, of course, that year it was also the day when the World Trade Center towers went down.

My good friends Joel and Dana on the Grand Canyon.

It was a strange time. As we packed the rafts and headed into the canyon, we were all worried about going off the grid because of the terrorist attacks only a week earlier. US flights had only resumed a few days before our flight to Arizona. There would be no phones, no Internet connections, and no communication available. What if something were to happen?

As we drifted down the river, the walls of rock rose higher around us, giving us a view of geology going back millions of years. In some ways, it was easy to imagine living in Afghanistan, and we wondered if

Osama bin Laden was hiding in similar terrain. It was somewhat surreal, given the world trauma, to be in this ageless place. The fear of an unseen enemy had penetrated our national border and had shifted our collective psyche. But we were now in sacred space, which gave us room to process in a different manner. We were moved by the gravity of our history, and we were drawn to be beacons of healing from the depths.

We traveled nearly 250 miles on our journey. The days consisted of pleasant drifts and paddles, punctuated by rapids of varying intensity. The river and its course set the mood of the day, some days giving us space to reflect and others requiring our full attention. We had four inflatable kayaks, called duckies, that the rafters could use and one guide in a kayak to help with the stragglers. I befriended the kayak guide and convinced him to share his ride. Over the course of a couple of weeks, I paddled the biggest water I'd ever experienced.

Our river days also included some incredible hikes in the side canyons. We'd find an amazing place to camp and set up shop, and we'd usually have some free hours to explore at the end of the day. I loved climbing up into the canyon walls, which were full of surprises. The plant and bird life was remarkable, and the rock formations, weathered by water, were mind-boggling. By the time we got to the deepest part of the canyon, we had descended 1.8 billion years in geological time. We did some group work talking about the world and what was happening and what we could do for our community. I was moved to bring it home, to use

Hollyhock friends Eduardo and Gloria Schwartz with Drummond Pike at the helm.

this timely journey and what it did for me to bring healing to our city, to our neighborhood, to the people in my circle.

This experience, looking through the lens of healing during these fragile times, led to a deepening of work through and with the Village Fund. Our focus shifted toward social justice, and we looked for ways where we could promote healing here at home. We looked to partner with some of the Nashville "saints," those who do healing work with people on the edge. We deepened support of Becca Stevens and Magdalene, a residential community for women who have survived lives of violence and prostitution. With the creation of Becca's social enterprise, Thistle Farms, these inspiring women have had a chance to work creating lotions, bath products, and candles and an opportunity to find a new community and lifestyle. We also began supporting Room in the Inn, working with Father Strobel's organization to feed, house, and provide healing for the homeless. We supported the work of Conexión Américas, an organization led by Renata Soto, helping immigrant Latino families navigate the difficult challenge of learning to live in Middle Tennessee, far from home. These were trying times for the nation, and it felt good for me and our growing agent base to invest time and resources in things of great meaning to our community.

Nashville was now embracing more density, and developers started building more condominiums in the downtown and midtown. By 2003, our business had heated up with a multi-residential strategy, and we began to list developments such as the Enclave and Icon in the Gulch. That and the emergence of Core Development with our early project Werthan Mills Lofts provided new opportunities for the Village Fund. During each sale or development project, we looked for and found ways to leverage Village Fund so that both the business success of the project and the resulting community around the completed development would be enhanced.

For instance, the development team at Bomasada, a group out of Houston developing the Enclave in Hillsboro Village, had blundered in the community meetings and did not have a fan base. When they hired us to sell the project, I encouraged them to commit a donation per unit sale to the Village Fund for a pocket park at St. Bernard's. They did, and we collected $28,800 from them, as we sold out the 148-unit project. This move improved the relationship that they had with the community and had lasting impact, as the park can now be enjoyed by everyone.

Additionally, we worked with Bristol Development Group on several projects and listed the 420-unit Icon in the Gulch. Given that the Gulch was just beginning to emerge as Nashville's newest neighborhood at the time, we felt that we could use the listing, and the relationship, to make a long-term impact. We encouraged Bristol to co-fund with Village, as the listing agent, a master plan for a Gulch Greenway study. We jointly provided the funding for the study through the Village Fund. Sometimes things can take a while to emerge, and in this case, many years after completion of these projects, we are now witnessing the tangible end result of this early study.

In 2007, the Village Fund, with support from Core Development, funded a project in North Nashville that supported youth enrichment and urban art. The project was designed to create a mural the length of a football field. The Metropolitan Development and Housing Agency (MDHA) had a long, corrugated metal wall on Rosa Parks Boulevard that was stark and unattractive and a target for graffiti. It was begging for a mural. I contacted Watkins Institute, a nearby school for the arts, which referred me to artists who created a "numbers wall."

The numbers wall on Rosa Parks Boulevard across from Werthan Mills Lofts.

The Village Fund gave money to Community Friendship, Inc., a group that works with children in an educational mode. We hired the artists to come up with an urban mural concept and sketch it on the corrugated metal wall and recruited neighborhood children to paint the wall. The artists had numbered the wall so that each young artist could paint by number. Village agents joined in the painting, which went on over the course of the summer, and we were all amazed when our numbers merged into a beautiful urban mural. The mural is right across from Werthan Mills Lofts on Rosa Parks Boulevard and is still graffiti-free today, which seems to speak to a sense of neighborhood pride in the work. As if that wasn't thanks enough, Village and Community Friendship, Inc. were unexpectedly given an award from the Mayor's Office for neighborhoods and community engagement.

I love how the Village Fund fosters awareness within our agent community. Now with over two hundred approved nonprofits that we've supported, our agents can focus on a particular area of passion and become the face of Village within that organization. Our "Change Agents" program spotlights our agents who are doing such outstanding community work. We hear about their work at our sales meetings and promote them both internally and externally.

In 2014 we had a special "Million Points of Light" celebration, as the fund had passed the $1 million mark in moving funds back to the community. As I prepared to take the stage to name the recipients of the 2014 Village Fund grants, I had a moment. Some people call it "spacing out" or "zoning out" or even "going to another place." I just couldn't believe what this little fund had created. With over three hundred guests in the room, including representatives from over eighty nonprofits, I was emotional, and all that I could say was, "A lot of a little is a lot."

Afterward, I milled through the crowd, which included many of our agents. We all carried a sense of pride about what we'd achieved together, and the gathering and the response from our guests fortified us for our next round of work. Talking with representatives from the nonprofits, I listened to updates on their work and heard from them how important our support and partnership had been to them through the years. The Village Fund is now funding faster, nearing the $2 million mark, and we brought the funds back home to the Community Foundation of Middle Tennessee.

Jenn Garrett and Brian Copeland of Village present award to Brian Williams and the team of Hands on Nashville. (L to R: Garrett, Copeland, Samantha Hart, Jaclyn Mothupi, Mark Deutschmann, Williams.)

I have learned many lessons along the way, from my work with Hollyhock, from SVN and some of the amazing members, and from many of the nonprofit leaders here at home. Through the years, I've gained more experience and understanding of how the work that I do, when coupled with others, impacts our community. Starting with selling homes—and, if you haven't gotten it yet, "I sell homes within a one-mile radius of Hillsboro Village"—I was doing what I considered to be good work. I was supporting and enhancing the neighborhood commercial districts, working with and shaping area nonprofits, and leveraging partnerships in a way that was making a tangible difference.

How does all this happen? Well, I have come up with some ingredients that are useful when considering impact, ideas that can shape and evolve community within a one-mile radius. These things have a ripple effect and over time can influence and give flavor to the broader community and perhaps to a city and beyond.

1. **EVOLVING COMMERCIAL DISTRICTS.** Need space for community to gather. Commercial districts are the epicenter of a walkable neighborhood.

2. **LEADERSHIP.** Someone has to take charge. There are always the "issues of the day" and tasks that must be tackled in the community.

3. **SHARED VISION.** People need to find a common goal. This includes neighborhood identity, how we see ourselves, and what we want to become.

4. **POLITICAL WILL.** Gaining support from public officials is key. Elect public officials who support the health of our urban centers.

5. **CIVIC ENGAGEMENT.** Roll up one's sleeves and get involved. Groups like the Nashville Civic Design Center (NCDC), the Urban Land Institute (ULI), Greenways for Nashville (GfN), Hands On Nashville (HON), and Affordable Housing Resources (AHR) are flexible, evolving, and can be leveraged to impact change.
6. **CONNECTION** and ability to pull other like-minded groups to the table. It takes a village, and sometimes more is better. If a cause is important, different groups can impact in their unique way.
7. **PHILANTHROPY.** The Village Fund provides a good example of this philosophy. The Community Foundation is a bigger tool. Focused, sustained giving at the local level is powerful.
8. **NATURAL RESOURCES.** Greenways and public spaces can be activated. Look for the natural assets that can be pulled into service. Lean and green is becoming a topic of the day, and we can work to better our collective urban health.
9. **DEVELOPMENT.** Adaptive reuse and in-fill concepts are essential for smart growth. We need to espouse the responsible use of our land. Core Development and others can use tools and resources to create the built environment.
10. **MARKETING AND SALES.** It is important to share the vision and to bring in others. The Village team of Change Agents can truly create collective buy-in, key to enhancing a neighborhood.

Chapter 4

Committing to Community

How much connection did you just make? That is one way to measure whether or not the work you did made a difference.

—Seth Godin,
The Icarus Deception

WHEN VILLAGE WAS in its formative stages, Bill Clinton was in office, and Hillary had just come out with the book *It Takes a Village*. She was referring, of course, to the wisdom of an old proverb: it takes a village to create community, to effectively run a community, and to take care of its people. I'm with her. Though most real estate companies in Nashville were named after their founder, I was reasonably certain that Deutschmann's Real Estate Services wouldn't fly. People wouldn't join a company if they couldn't even pronounce the name, let alone spell it. So I chose the name Village Real Estate Services, knowing that it takes a village to build community.

I wanted more than the status quo for our real estate family, and we wanted a new definition of community, one that meant we were inclusive and generous—that we would give to those around us and take part in creating the neighborhoods and the city of our dreams. This helped me identify the kind of community in which I wanted to live, the kind of businessman I could be and how I wanted to shape my life. The foundation for this work often comes from being part of a loving family that teaches you how to care for one another and models how to be in the community. As anyone would extend a hand to help a relative in crisis, we likewise reach out to one another when our community is in need.

Nashville has been impacted by two natural disasters that have shaped the growth of our city in recent years and relate to connections in community. One of them was the tornado that ripped through the city in 1998, two years after Village's incorporation. While I was showing customers property under some very dark clouds near Centennial Park, my mother called from Maryland to inform me that CNN was reporting a tornado. The tornado touched down on Charlotte Avenue, stormed through Centennial Park, headed downtown, jumped the river, and slammed into East Nashville. Hundreds of homes were severely damaged, and over six thousand mature trees were snapped or uprooted. At the time, Village was starting to sell lots of homes and neighborhood commercial properties in that area. In fact, just the day before the storm, I had closed on the property that now houses the Lipstick Lounge.

I was worried for our customers and set out to survey the damaged neighborhoods of our hometown. I made it over to East Nashville after midnight and found shocked friends and neighborhood customers standing in front of rubble that used to be their homes. With so many trees thrown across the roads, it was hard to navigate, but I made it to the building that I'd just closed on, only to find it no longer had a roof.

On Woodland Street, I talked to a couple whose home I was listing. They were drinking wine on their neighbor's front stoop, looking back at their front porch, which had been crushed by a falling tree. They shrugged their shoulders and said they were just thankful they weren't hurt. And, they said with wry humor, this probably would delay the sale.

This natural disaster had a huge impact on the community. Nashville rose to the occasion, and neighborhood activists set the stage for transformation. The Regional/Urban Design Assistance Team (R/UDAT), led by Hunter Gee, was formed to provide tools for assessing community needs and a vision for the future. ReLeaf Nashville, a program created by the Nashville Tree Foundation, raised $1,000,000 in six months and, with a host of volunteers, replanted two thousand trees in East Nashville alone, most of which were native species.

Prior to the storm, East Nashville had a high percentage of rundown properties, many of them owned by ... well, by slumlords. There is just no other word for them. After the storm, R/UDAT was able to require these terrible landlords to bring their properties up to code or suffer the penalties. That, coupled with an abundance of insurance money, led to home repairs and the removal of unsightly blight. Renovators also began buying up houses in the area and upgrading them, improving the neighborhood.

The infusion of capital led to additional, opportunistic development in the area, and many new businesses emerged. In late 1998, Village joined the movement by buying Renaissance Real Estate Company and moving to Woodland Street alongside a number of other new merchants. Local developers saw an opportunity and bought and renovated neighborhood commercial properties. It didn't take long before Bongo Java, Margot Café, Marché, and the Red Door Saloon landed in Five Points.

At the time, local community leaders such as Christine Kreyling, Eileen Beehan, Ann Roberts, and Diane Neighbors led campaigns to beautify streets, improve the schools, and enforce building and zoning codes, and they worked with the Metropolitan Government of Nashville to focus both money and attention to the area. Other investors soon added to the momentum, helping to fund the start of new businesses, including Rosepepper Cantina, the Turnip Truck, Chapel Bistro, and the Family Wash. Social events such as the popular Tomato Festival started and successfully pulled throngs of people across the river to experience the area's unique character. Residential real estate sales and renovations continued to boost the eclectic mix of engaged residents.

Today East Nashville continues to boom, and the impact is spreading. Five Points has continued to see resurgence, with developers such as Mark Sanders leading the way. Other leaders, like March Egerton and Dan Heller, have continued to invest in the neighborhood, and the transformation of Riverside Village and Gallatin Pike are enhancing the neighborhood commercial mix. Core Development has projects in Three Points and in Rosebank, while Woodland Street Partners is one of many developers creating an abundance of good in-fill housing. Village agents are in Cleveland Park, Highland

Heights, South Inglewood, Rosebank, and other East Nashville neighborhoods that are continuing to evolve.

Though the tornado was a destructive force, it ultimately brought out the best in this community, focusing and accelerating its evolution. It was a very important lesson that chaos—natural, personal, or otherwise—is sometimes necessary for change. With a great community, even disasters are catalysts for the transformation that needs to happen.

As East Nashville was healing and transforming after the tornado, I met John Knott in a strange twist of fate. Village was beginning to export our multi-residential sales experience to other cities, and we were selling a seventy-two-unit condo project, Bee Street Lofts, in Charleston, South Carolina, for a developer we'd worked with in Nashville. Beth Vincent, a Village agent traveling to the project, met John at the airport. She had witnessed another traveler leaving garbage in his wake and had tidied up after him. As she tossed the mess in the trash bin, John saw her and said, "It's a wonder how some people live." They struck up a conversation, and he told her about his project in North Charleston called Noisette. Beth recommended that John and I meet.

John is one of the three influential leaders in the world of development that carry on the legacy of James Rouse, the developer of Columbia, Maryland, where I spent my formative years. John, who is a senior fellow at the Urban Land Institute (ULI), is an inspiring man with a big vision. I met John, and he described himself as a "community builder," a term that really struck a chord.

At that time, John was working as a master developer of North Charleston and had purchased and controlled the 360-acre riverside property Noisette, a former navy yard. They had gone through a massive development process with the community, detailing the ten thousand-year history of the area, the major natural assets, the community attributes, and the local talent. We visited John regularly throughout that year, and I was moved by his contributions to the community.

After meeting John and hearing how he identified himself, I have also come to see myself as a community builder. My work—selling homes, creating households, improving neighborhood commercial districts, developing communities, working with local nonprofits, participating as a change maker, and collaborating with local politic—has, and continues to have, an impact on the community.

When it comes to community building, family comes first. What you create in your home can mirror who you are in the larger world around you. Though I came alone to Nashville in 1985, I knew that the first part of making a community was making a family.

When Chelsea was born in 1989, my first wife, K-Lea, and I decided we wanted to raise our child with the support of our extended network. We'd recently been to Maui to visit Chelsea's grandmother and were impressed with the way some of the islanders raised their kids. Often, it was hard to figure out who the child's parents were. The kids ran from lap to lap. The entire community had their eyes out, watching if the kids got out of hand, administering discipline when needed, and giving love, always. I liked the concept and wanted to adopt the way of life.

We decided to have our own version of this—a sort of baptism by community—for Chelsea, with a circle of friends, passing her around for all to cherish. Chelsea was in the middle of a lot of circles and made a lot of friends. She was in real estate circles, yoga circles, drum circles, juggling circles, and was involved in some of the other esoteric teachings, like Alaya, that we were exploring. She even befriended various neighborhood families and was invited to church, temple, and other gatherings with them. She called them her church families. It's no wonder that she got an environmental studies degree, and is now attending divinity school at Naropa in Boulder. Whatever we did worked. Chelsea has grown up to be a community builder and has friends and extended family who welcome her in wherever she goes.

Over time, and particularly after Sherry and I married, family members started moving to Nashville, including nephews and nieces, sisters and brothers, and they in turn created families of their own. Daniel Harris, my sister's son, was first, coming to Nashville after high school to intern at Village. Daniel later attended Vanderbilt and worked his way into the Vanderbilt baseball program, becoming director of baseball operations while still a student and continuing in that role for a few years after he graduated, in the years that Vanderbilt went to the College World Series. He then moved on to LetterLogic and enjoys a robust career in sales. Other nieces and nephews followed. Nashville is very enticing. Residents may leave for a time, but they tend to come back. We are apparently attracting eighty-eight people per day to our city, many of whom are millennials choosing place before career. Some are like my family: family members attracting other family members from other places.

My mother also relocated here. At eighty-seven years old, she's semi-independent and lives in St. Paul's Senior Community, tucked in the Green Hills neighborhood, which is the perfect place for her. I soon discovered that the mothers of two of my favorite Democrats, Stewart Clifton and former mayor Bill Purcell, also resided here. We all decided to have a lunch with our mothers and, given that the first lunch was on Good Friday, called it Good Mothers, Good Sons,

Good Friday. We maintained the tradition for a couple of years, and had a Good Mothers, Good Sons lunch every month.

Our lunches always centered on family and politics. We generally had a check-in about our family happenings and then moved to some central political issue. My mother has little interest in the local political scene but had to tolerate some conversation among the Good Sons, who are quite engaged locally. She usually interrupted and forced us onto a national or international topic, such as the presidential race or the impact of falling oil prices. She was sorely disappointed if we wasted too much of our precious time on lesser subjects.

Mark and Rebel throwing eight clubs in Centennial Park.

While community building starts with the family, it can take many forms, and we each shape our community in our own unique way. Just as I encourage my agents to have a USP (unique selling proposition), we all shape our world and our work in the ways that we engage in community. It doesn't really matter which community that you engage, everyone loves to talk about home at some level, and engagement means that you have that potential to create a customer—the precursor to a successful sales career—without even really trying.

Joining an extracurricular activity or peer network is an excellent way to engage with teammates, neighbors, and friends in a deeper way than business alone can do. And it is a great way to create a network. If you look for something you love to do, you can show another authentic side of yourself, have fun, and enjoy some fresh air and exercise, while experiencing the beauty of where you live at the same time.

One of my early Nashville customers was a professor, Laura Novick, who moved to Vanderbilt from Stanford and bought a house in the Hillsboro Village neighborhood. I was pleased to discover that Laura was an accomplished juggler, skilled in intricate club passing patterns. We teamed up and founded the Nashville Juggling Club, setting regular Tuesday evening meetings in Centennial Park.

Over time, the club became quite robust, and throughout the 1990s it attracted some very good jugglers. Carter Andrews emerged from the mix, noting that he'd had a version of a juggling club in the past, and sometimes dropped in. Rebel Bailey and I had a running bet, $5 whenever we dropped—and we were passing eight clubs with triple spins! He still owes me. One notable juggler, Robert Nelson, moved from San Francisco for a few years (also buying a home through me!). Robert, a.k.a. Butterfly Man, with a beautiful butterfly tattoo on his bald forehead, was famous for his work, and was known as the King of Pier 39. He did a raucous, off-color performance, and routinely did a seven-ball reverse cascade in his act, saying, "I do it backward, just to piss other jugglers off."

Laura, a professorial brainiac, was big on club-passing routines and put together some intricate group patterns. I preferred the more spontaneous moves and particularly loved to "feed" a three-person free-for-all, where everyone throws their "s--t"; left-hand doubles, triples, overhand, whirly birds, reverses, over the shoulders, and around the backs. As long as they got 'em close, I was reasonably capable of incorporating them into the pattern, and send the club back out—often with my own "s--t" to keep them off balance.

Juggling can truly build communities. Our club was affiliated with a larger organization, the International Jugglers' Association (IJA), dedicated to promoting juggling. The IJA was created in 1947 to answer the need for "an organization for jugglers that would provide meetings at regular intervals in an atmosphere of mutual friendship." Members range from top professionals to avid hobbyists.

One of the IJA's claims to fame is its annual juggling festival, held in a different North American city every year. I have attended a dozen or so of these festivals in my time. The festivals attract over a thousand people each year, offering special workshops for developing new skills and parading jugglers through the host city. The festival culminates in the national competition, featuring individual championships, numbers competition, renegade shows, and even a marathon (running and juggling, called joggling). I took Chelsea to the festival in Baltimore when she was just three weeks old. We were in the audience when Anthony Gotto, a child prodigy who had grown up in Ellicott City, Maryland near us at the Homewood House, juggled five clubs continuously and without a drop for forty-five minutes, setting the Guinness world record. Every year there is a big group photo, the "big throw up," where the jugglers throw everything in the air at once. It would be great to bring the festival to Nashville. I've not asked, but I bet that we could.

Our club evolved, and one of our members, Jacob Weiss, founded the Vanderbilt Juggling and Physical Arts program, whose members include students, faculty, staff, and other members of the community, including some from the Nashville Juggling Club. This group has put on an annual production, Juggleville, since 2005. Juggleville combines themed juggling, dance, acrobatics, and comedy—a very entertaining show. It is also unique in that it pulls in both the novice three-ball juggler and the highly skilled performer in a way that really works.

Juggling kept me balanced in my work with Village. I actually found a couple of booking agents to hire me out and did what I could to ace the job. Eldon and Kathy Bale (yes, they also bought a home through me) booked me in the music industry, one of the benefits of being a juggler in Music City. I was hired to juggle at the fortieth birthday party of Warner CEO and music industry veteran Jim Ed Norman, who I learned was also a juggler. I juggled for the Oak Ridge Boys at their celebrity softball game. I regularly juggled at concerts at the old Starwood Amphitheatre, including an Eric Clapton performance. My favorite music gig of all time was at the Theatre Knoxville Downtown, where I was the act between bands. Bela Fleck, Sam Bush, and Tony Rice performed on that Halloween night, and I did a rendition of the Danger Man routine, juggling knives, bottles, and fire to fit the theme.

Another booking agent, Chuckles the Clown, thought that all of his performers should be clowns. So, I developed my character and became a juggling clown in TV commercials for various brands including Toyota, Ford, and Kroger. I was the Kroger clown when the company decided to sell do-it-yourself pizzas and was filmed for the great pizza-making challenge. We filmed in Memphis, and I juggled every ingredient imaginable, including sausages, tomatoes, and, of course, machetes. Unfortunately, I had an accident at 3 a.m. and had to make a visit to the emergency room. The producers adapted to the injury, and I showed up in the next shot, imploring the audience with a big bandaged finger to "be careful." And yes, I later sold the producer, Bob Cummins, and his wife their home.

That was not the only time machetes got me into hot water. I performed downtown at Summer Lights, an annual Nashville festival between Public Square and the War Memorial building on Deaderick. The streets were closed off for the festival, and I got a permit to busk. I worked the crowds, bringing kids and adults into my performances, and I passed the hat. Once, a man jumped into my act, picked up my machetes, and started to juggle. Within a few throws, he had cut a big gash in his hand and was off to the emergency room, where he got twenty-three stitches. He was shocked. "I didn't know that they were sharp!" he said.

"I didn't ask you to juggle them," I replied.

Years later, I worked at the Tennessee Renaissance Festival, a Shakespearian/Old English festival complete with a castle, which has now been around for thirty years. I took on an Old English accent and did themed juggling for that event. Coincidentally, I bumped into an act called the Singing Executioners, a hilarious and gaudy performance. Talking with them afterward, I realized that one of the two guys was the man who'd interfered in my juggling act at Summer Lights, and he showed me the long scar on his hand.

Juggling for the Special Olympics, in the Vanderbilt University football stadium, I had another accident. I was performing with one of my favorite artists, John Hartford ("Gentle on My Mind"), and had planned a pretty good act. I had an eight-foot inflatable ball ready to bounce down through the crowd, at the same time I planned to juggle three forty-eight-inch beach balls. Unfortunately, I worked the machetes first, and caught a blade. But the show must go on, and blood was flying as I juggled the beach balls to the oohs and aahs of that special crowd. Maybe I should dull the blades.

Juggling allowed me to approach the community and build community in a completely different way. It created a dynamic relationship with those around me. They didn't just see me as a "real estate guy" but could relate to me in a personal, fun way that I think expanded and deepened the business.

Participating in team sports is another way to interact with and build community. In the early 1990s, I hired Danny Petraitis, who worked with PLA Media, to help me strengthen my real estate practice with the music industry. As I have noted, Music Row was in my "one-mile radius," and many in the music business were already customers. Danny invited me to network at a corporate music event and introduced me to the event photographer, Tim Campbell, who was also Danny's teammate and longtime member of the softball team called the Scattered Showers. Tim, the captain, invited me to my first practice. I've always loved baseball, having played on teams since early childhood, and I was psyched.

Tim Buppert and Tim Campbell of the Scattered Showers.

The team was already well seasoned, with a bunch of crazy guys who knew each other from high school and who were still playing after nearly twenty years. The team, though very competitive and playing in the Metro Nashville Softball Association, favored longevity over skill, thus it was hard to break in. Practice was on Sunday at 9 a.m., so it favored those willing to forgo morning services—perfect for a preacher's kid. When I earned my position in left field, I was able to hold on for over a decade. I loved these softball games, generally held at 7 p.m. at the softball fields in Shelby Bottoms. Our team featured Myles Maillie, an eccentric artist who was our shortstop. Myles, a painter, designed our shirts, and given that he gave me number sixty-six, my nickname became Root. Marc Rossi, our second baseman, was a model for consistency. Robert Fitters, who shared the outfield with me, was one of the original Showers.

We were very close and always had dinner at Brown's Diner together after the games. We communed when members of the Showers held other social events, most notably at the Myles Maillie Christmas Bus Party, an annual winter holiday event. Tim and Myles lived on the same street in Waverly Belmont, so Tim would host a potluck, and Myles would host the after party, catering a couple of buses to carry the party to late-night jazz clubs and honky-tonks in urban neighborhoods across the city. Myles is a crazy guy, and there was never a bus party without incident.

Tim Campbell, our third basemen, was a spiritual leader of the team. He held the team together in later years when most of us would have naturally retired. When Tim died of cancer in 2011, the team drifted apart. We had a last gathering at my home when Tim was dying, and each of us shared heartfelt passion for our teammate and for our dear old Scattered Showers. Over the years, the team became much more than a bunch of guys playing a game. We were full of camaraderie and community—a band of brothers.

It's important to be involved not only with fun community groups but also with business communities and peer groups. I got involved with the Nashville Civic Design Center (NCDC) to help Nashville think about smart growth, good design guidelines, and the redevelopment of our evolving urban neighborhoods, and served on the board for a number of years. Under the guidance of Mark Schimmenti, the original executive director for the organization, and Gary Gaston, the assistant director, the group put together a series of design charrettes. In these community meetings, held in nine urban neighborhoods in and around downtown, staff led groups of neighbors through a process of re-envisioning their neighborhood. Eight to ten neighbors were grouped at numerous tables with a big area map to study. They were encouraged to talk through a series of issues as a team and to map out what they wanted. These maps, when completed, became a community-designed outlook for schools, parks, neighborhood commercial areas, and other ideas that emerged.

I attended most of these events and learned a lot about what the citizens of our city wanted for their communities. These events allowed everyone the opportunity to be a community builder and to have a voice. The charrettes were well attended, and neighbors were passionate about designing for their future.

Gary Gaston of the NCDC leads the neighborhood charrettes for the Plan of Nashville.

In North Nashville I attended the charrette across from the old and vacant Werthan bag factory. These neighbors said loud and clear that they were tired of being known as the crime district. They were interested in economic development on Rosa Parks and Jefferson Streets and also wanted mixed-income housing. I was impressed that every table circled the Werthan bag factory on their maps, noting their desire for these buildings to become artists' lofts. I tucked that information away, knowing that it would influence my work in the years to come.

NCDC charrette participants compiled these neighborhood discussions and came back with a major presentation about what they had heard. They followed this, in 2005, with an amazing book titled *The Plan of Nashville*. Modeled after *Plan of Chicago*, published a century earlier, the Nashville book was designed to take the city forward for the next fifty years.

The book proposed the following ten design principles:

1. Respect Nashville's natural and built environment.
2. Treat the Cumberland River as central to Nashville's identity.
3. Reestablish the streets as the principal public space of community and connectivity.
4. Develop a convenient and efficient transportation infrastructure.
5. Provide for a comprehensive, interconnected greenway and park system.
6. Develop an economically viable downtown district as the heart of the region.
7. Raise the quality of the public realm with civic structures and spaces.
8. Integrate public art into the design of the city, its buildings, public works, and parks.
9. Strengthen the unique identity of neighborhoods.
10. Infuse visual order into the city by strengthening sight lines to and from civic landmarks and natural features.

These principles have served Nashville well. The NCDC emerged as one of the premier community building organizations in our city and has influenced the recreation of our riverfront park system, our urban greenways, and our public art. It has also strengthened the unique identity of many of our emerging neighborhoods.

I also joined the Urban Land Institute (ULI), an organization that's redeveloping neighborhoods and cities around the globe and, most importantly, developing leaders in those neighborhoods to further the mission. Nashville created a ULI chapter in 2008, with the support and leadership of Bert Mathews and Hunter Gee. The ULI's mission statement begins with the phrase "To provide leadership in the responsible use of land," which is intertwined with nearly every aspect of the organization. We challenge our members to be leaders in their communities, their fields, and the ULI by creating sustainable and thriving communities worldwide.

I became a member of the ULI's Nashville chapter, a great group which now has over five hundred developers, architects, engineers, and others in the development world who are interested in Nashville's smart growth. When I joined, I promised Bert that I'd give it a try and to be involved for at least one year. Now, years later, I became the chair of mission advance, which meant that I served on the executive team and helped our group plan our topics. At ULI, we explore issues such as building healthy corridors and affordable housing, trail-oriented development, and the emergence of urban magnets. We ensure that our content is relevant and current. What we do in the ULI contributes to the growth of our city today. I became chairperson of the organization in July 2017 and will preside over the ULI national spring conference in Nashville in 2019.

As Nashville continues to evolve, it's important that the conversations and discussions shaping the communities push forward, too. The ULI Nashville has become a voice in Nashville's evolution and is a great vehicle for building on the good in our community. Mayor Barry asked ULI to chart out recommendations for her infrastructure plan for the city, and we engaged Gabe Klein, the author of *Start-Up City*, to preside over our local team. My friend and ULI member Kim Hawkins, who I have since appointed as the chair of mission advance, organized the local team. Gabe ran the Zipcar office in Washington, D.C., before being hired to be D.C.'s director of transportation. Later, he became the transportation commissioner under Mayor Raul Emanuel in Chicago. In these bureaucratic roles, Gabe showed the initiative, intuition, and common sense necessary to get things done. His motto in Chicago? Chicago: Getting Shit Done.

In 2016, when the Metro Council was contemplating mandatory inclusionary zoning, the ULI hosted several key affordable housing discussions. Notable was a discussion with Jonathan Rose, a rock star based in New York City who has been building affordable housing for many years. This event, titled "You Can Build Affordable Housing," featured both a local panel and a keynote address from Jonathan. Jonathan shared his experience with public/private partnership, and showed our development community and public officials some of the tools that he has utilized in his career to build stellar affordable and mixed-income projects.

It was a timely exchange, because Nashville is experiencing growth in all real estate sectors. *Business Insider* named Nashville the hottest city in the nation in 2015 and 2016. There is so much construction that there is a "Crane Watch" in the Nashville Business Journal. We are seeing downtown offices, office buildings, and residential construction throughout the downtown and midtown and in our suburban office centers.

However, along with affordable housing, I noted at the meeting, Nashville now lacks a good supply of the upper end, "lock and leave" for sale housing. There are over four thousand households in MLS Area 2 with residents who have lived in their homes for fifteen years, are over fifty years of age, and who have over an acre to service. Where will they move when they decide to forgo home maintenance if they want to age in our community? This population, like the millennials, likes the convenience and walkability of the city. Almost all of the higher-end housing in the urban core in the last development cycle, from 2008 to present, has been rental product. At the time of this writing, new for sale empty-nester housing, with right-sized units for an aging population, is really only available at resale projects like 1212 in the Gulch. And with projects on the horizon like CityLights and perhaps the 505, more will be needed to satisfy demand.

But the shadow side to all of this success, the panelists noted, is that housing is becoming less affordable. The average rent in Nashville is up 18 percent since 2009, at a pace among the fastest in the nation. Affordable housing seems to be the mantra among many groups like Nashville Organized for Action and Hope (NOAH), but at the same time there is resistance in many neighborhoods to development and growth, even along corridors. Urban neighborhoods are gentrifying, and some are experiencing a wholesale teardown and rebuild. Live/make, live/work districts are on the forefront as we look to service our creatives. There is an urgent need for attainable and workforce housing, and a first-pass mandatory inclusionary zoning has made it through the Metropolitan Council. The Barnes Fund for Affordable Housing had largely been symbolic until Mayor Barry promised $10 million in grant funding in both the 2016 and 2017 capital budgets, with another $25 million in 2017 set aside to buy low-income housing to stabilize rents.. Nashville needs to keep an eye on the quality of life and to remember those who made us cool. Community is about all sectors, not just the people who can afford it.

Afterward, at Jonathan Rose's event, he signed copies of his book *A Well-Tempered City*, in which he explores what modern science, ancient civilizations, and human nature can teach us about the future of urban life. He describes the entanglement of cities, and how people, buildings, neighborhoods, and businesses are entwined with each other, and talks about how to create community fitness. Affordable housing is a key component in creating community fitness. I was honored to spend some time with Jonathan, and to introduce him at the event. He seemed familiar to me, and I realized that he was an early SVN member and that, like me, he'd created his business as a result of the influence of that organization.

Furthering my involvement in community, and while continuing to be involved in SVN, in 2012 I joined the local chapter of the Entrepreneurs' Organization (EO), which is basically a support group for entrepreneurs that offers training, peer feedback, and access to vendors and services for people with growing businesses and high revenue.

There are 144 chapters in forty-six countries, so it is a global organization that acts locally. The EO has been deeply involved with the Nashville Entrepreneur Center, a hub for entrepreneurial support, through the Catalyst program. EOers act as mentors for these burgeoning entrepreneurs and give them an opportunity for the next level of peer support when their businesses grow.

One of the most valuable features of the EO is its forum, which is designed to create a safe environment for sharing all aspects of business and life. Our forum, Forum 12, is comprised of eight local entrepreneurs. The EO promises that your forum members are going to become your friends and allies, and it is true. We follow the EO rules of engagement, the most important of which is forum confidentiality. What happens in forum stays in the forum. This is crucial if members are going to truly share challenges and issues.

Mark and his EO forum buddies in San Miguel de Allende, Mexico. From left to right: Darek Bell, Alan Young, Peter Hermann, Allen Baler, Adam James, Max Goldberg, Mark, and Bill Kimberlin.

One of the first things that we did in forum training was to create and share our lifeline. A lifeline shows the key turning points in our life and how each incident, event, or relationship shaped our lives. It's an expression of the pattern that connects us from birth to present. We shared this with each other to gain a better group understanding of who we are, where we came from, and what we wanted to become.

Our experience has been augmented by what is called the Forum Retreat, when we take three to four days for a focused excursion. Our first retreat featured a big houseboat on the lake, which gave us plenty of time for structured activity, plus additional time for fishing, swimming, and revelry. Usually we travel and have now held retreats in Fort Lauderdale, Austin, and San Miguel de Allende.

On one of our retreats, we decided to do some fly-fishing in the Smoky Mountains. Bill Kimberlin, one of the Forum 12 creatives, managed to rustle up a full-size tour bus for our journey, and we toured in style to the mountains. What we didn't count on was winding mountain roads as we neared our cabin and found ourselves off-road without a viable turnaround. Mountain folks seem to be suspicious and did not treat us kindly when we tried to turn around. The people came out to view the spectacle, some sporting firearms. We tried to be inconspicuous, which is impossible in a long sleek vehicle, and pulled in to some private property. I tried to remove a chain to give us the room to turn around but was greeted with hostility. We were prohibited entry, and Bill, who was our driver of the day, had to make a harrowing three-point turn, with about two hundred adjustments, under the watchful eye of the locals, and some serious embankments on the side to maneuver. We never reached the cabin in that bus and had to solicit other local help to get there. We did have one day of fly-fishing but were really so relieved that we just chilled for the rest of the journey. This bus incident felt like a metaphor for what we run into in business. We may be sporting a team attitude and community building, but the locals have to be in on it, too.

My forum, Forum 12, happens to be all guys: Allen, Alan, Adam, Darek, Pete, Max, and Bill. We are all local entrepreneurs, so our paths do occasionally cross in the business world. We have to balance our work together with our real purpose: to be there for each other. Darek Bell, of Corsair, for instance, has decided to locate his local whiskey production and a tasting room in Wedgewood Houston, across the street from The Finery, which my company Core Development is creating, and Max Goldberg has opened Bastion, one of his restaurants, down the street. The relationship with local entrepreneurs at the EO has opened many doors for the members. It's a true testament to how involvement in local organizations, non-profits, and neighborhood groups can deepen your connection in the community. Maybe the best part is when community and family and work merge together and the boundaries of this trilogy fall away.

When my wife Sherry and I met in 2004, we discovered that we'd arrived in Nashville at nearly the same time and that we'd been neighbors for nearly twenty years. We came to realize that she'd tried to buy no fewer than seven homes from me (through other agents) and that each time I'd sold the home from under her. She had also tried to buy property on 12South, right across the street from one of our early purchases. She claims that she watched me juggle and busk at Summer Lights. We had been in the same local circle all that time, yet our paths hadn't formally crossed.

When Sherry talks about how we met, she usually starts by saying, "I got his number off the bathroom wall." That's a true story. She was at Mafiaoza's in 12South with her daughter, Whitney, who was trying to convince her mother to sell her single-family home and buy a condo. Whitney came out of the restroom saying, "Mom, stall three, check it out and call that guy."

I've noted that one really has the undivided attention of the potential customer in front of bathroom urinals and in bathroom stalls, so I use an advertising company called Graffiti to market various projects to take advantage of these situations. At that time, I was advertising Kress Lofts, and Sherry called me (this time directly) to inquire.

We met downtown the next day, and I took her through the dilapidated old building, sharing my vision for the project. Sherry, who has a knack for design, had a more refined vision and bought out the Westview, a ten-unit boutique condo project with an amazing green roof that I was marketing. It took quite a while for the project to complete, and when we closed in early 2005, Sherry and I went back to Mafiaoza's to celebrate.

I asked Sherry to marry me on the last day of 2007, while we were in San Miguel de Allende in Mexico. I'd decided to honor my grandfather, Robert Graetz, who was born on December 31, and pop the question on his birthday. What I didn't know was that Sherry, who was impatient with the long dating game, had decided to end the relationship if I hadn't proposed before the end of the year. She had not shared that with me, of course, and I was surprised that she cried when I asked her to marry me on the morning of the thirty-first. She later told me her side of the story, and I am ever grateful that my grandfather was not born on January 1.

In 2010 Sherry and I signed up for "Real Speaking," an intensive public speaking workshop with Gail Larsen in Santa Fe. Both Sherry and I were emerging as leaders, which offers regular opportunities to speak, and we wanted to improve our game. I had launched Go Green, was involved in Greenways for Nashville, and held a leadership position at GNR, all of which required stepping out in front of an audience. Sherry had been selected Ernst and Young's Entrepreneurial Winning Woman, had received an international award from the Women's President Organization, was engaged as a mentor at the Entrepreneur Center, and was a guest speaker teaching classes at Vanderbilt. She felt a real passion for public speaking and felt that she could take it to the next level.

Sherry on the floor at LetterLogic.

Real Speaking is designed to help people discover their core message while learning some of the keys to success as a speaker. During the course of the workshop, we were invited to tell our story. Sherry, in one workshop speech, told us that she never went to college. She grew up as a Jehovah's Witness, a member of a Christian sect that doesn't regard schooling as important. She noted that knocking on doors as a Jehovah's Witness was the best sales training available; lots of doors are closed before one opens. She then talked about her company and how she started LetterLogic in her basement. She ended by stating her company motto, "Status Quo Sux" (SQS), demonstrating to us how she used this to inspire LetterLogic and herself. But this was not quite "it"; she was still looking for that core message.

One day, we did an exercise with magazines, poster board, glue, and scissors. We spent a couple of hours cutting and clipping, looking for pictures and words that might come together in a storyboard, something that would clue us in to that core message.

With her storyboard completed, Sherry stood up and said, "At LetterLogic, we put the employees first." That was a thought-provoking and powerful introduction. She had determined that her core message and purpose was to take care of her employees. Putting the employees first, she reasoned, and as her storyboard suggested, would be best for her customers. An engaged and happy workforce was the true reason that they offered superior service. This employee-centric business was what she'd been doing for years, and now it had a voice.

LetterLogic group shot in front of the corporate headquarters and factory.

LetterLogic is famous for its company culture. LetterLogic designs, fulfills, and mails patient-friendly statements for health care systems across the country and is dedicated to customer service. Sherry's secret sauce, though, is that the employees come first. All share 10 percent of the profits each month, equally. All get full health, dental, and life insurance benefits, bonuses for biking, walking, or taking public transportation to work, and regular rewards for good ideas—which are implemented. Sherry believes this is why the company is number one in customer service and why her customers pay a premium for what might be considered a commodity. The employees are empowered and therefore do inspired work, which cements customer loyalty. The LetterLogic Family Album, an annual tradition, is an inspiring collection of pictures, events, and quotes from the workforce.

Sherry has, in fact, taken public speaking to a new level. The emergence of her core message has led to public speaking gigs, and she is truly gifted. She is speaking for trade groups, entrepreneurial organizations, and women's business associations. The opportunities continued to evolve, as she was named in 2015 to the National Women's Business Council, a group that advises both the president and Congress. As an advocate for fair wages, Sherry attracted the attention of then secretary of labor and current chair of the Democratic National Committee, Tom Perez, and has been going to Washington for panels and testimony before Congress. She was honored in 2016 as a Champion of Change by the White House. She credits the emergence of her core message for much of this notoriety and knows that her voice, speaking up for women, will be more important than ever in the new administration.

'Sherry speaking, with Joel moderating, at the Social Venture Network at Hollyhock.

Mark Deutschmann is introduced as the new chairman of ULI. Photo by Jed DeKalb.

My Real Speaking storyboard consisted of pictures of urban density, surrounded by beautiful mountains, rivers, and natural beauty. At the heart of my work, I create community at the core and work to create vibrancy in the city, because I am an environmentalist concerned about the health of the planet. When I stood and delivered my speech, I started with "the core is the new edge" and described my work in those terms. Real Speaking asks that we come from a place of our core message whenever we have a chance to share with an audience.

I continue to believe that it takes a village, and I'm speaking regularly within my one-mile radius. I speak as president of GfN, as the new chairman of ULI, and quite regularly in the local business and real estate community. Speaking is one way to engage with and create community and to look for new ways to stand up and say what we believe. I feel lucky to be married to a strong leader who also feels strongly about investing in our vibrant community. We are a good team, MFEO (made for each other). She is part of my core, and together we build community.

And on a last note about building and fostering community relationships, in 2016 I was selected to participate in Leadership Nashville. Formed in 1976 by Nelson Andrews, Leadership Nashville describes itself as an independent, executive leadership program designed to give community leaders a three-dimensional view of the city. The goal is to build channels of communication between established leaders, to connect these leaders with community issues, and to equip participants with insights, not solutions. The men and women in my class of forty-four individuals represent a diversity of races, religions, ages, and political persuasions, as well as a geographical cross section of neighborhoods. At our opening retreat, I realized that Carter Andrews, son of the founder of this organization and also a seasoned juggler, was going to perform. Moments before his performance, he invited me to join him on the stage for a "juggle off," ninety seconds of throwing whatever we wanted to do. It was fun to be introduced to my new Leadership Nashville class in this way.

I learned of the workings of the organization first in 2014, when Sherry participated in the yearlong training. The group gathers monthly for a long day on a bus (there are forty-four members in each year's class because that's how many can fit on the bus), and each day has a theme. There is criminal justice day, when the group explores the court and penal systems; education day, exploring the different types of schools represented in our city; business day, exploring the business ecosystem from big business to start-ups; diversity day, exploring religious freedom and diversity; entertainment day, exploring music, tourism, and other important business in and for our city ... and more.

The organization is always very current and uses what is called the caucus—a moderated roundtable—to hear reactions and viewpoints from the group about what they have seen, learned, or decided to do after experiencing each day. The group is expected to be candid, and everyone is called to speak his mind. My year with Leadership Nashville expanded my horizons and made me a better community builder in our city. Committing to community is about maintaining your commitment to learn, to maintain the spirit of journey and adventure, even close to home.

2017 Leadership Nashville class at final retreat. Best class ever!

Chapter 5

Building a Thriving Core

Creativity is just connecting things.

—Steve Jobs

IN THE LATE 1980s, I was invited to join a troupe of jugglers in Nicaragua. We called ourselves "malabaristas por la paz," or "jugglers for peace," and the plan was to tour orphanages and hospitals in the area. I joined our troupe of four, led by Graham Ellis, in Managua, and we prepared our "acto." I had met Graham in early 1987, at the Hawaiian Juggler's Festival on the Big Island. Graham was an idealist—he founded a juggling commune called Bellyacres—and was a very good juggler and performer.

We were in war-torn Nicaragua, where the Sandinistas, backed by the Ortega government, were at war with the Contras, backed by the United States. Our troupe did not intend to engage politically; we were there for those who suffered as a result of the conflict, intending to bring some joy and laughter to the people, particularly the children who had lost loved ones.

Our plan went awry when we were invited to perform outside of the American embassy. A group of internationalists who were against the intervention were gathering to pay tribute to Ben Linder, who was the first North American killed by the Contras in the conflict. When our troupe performed at the event, we brought down the house—not because we were that good but because, we were told, Ben Linder was also a juggler.

Malabaristas por La Paz in Nicaragua.

It turns out that Ben Linder was a hydroelectric engineer, working to restore a system in Bocay. But he was also known as the juggler who dressed as a clown to get the kids to follow him into the clinic for vaccinations. The internationalists talked about a five-day hike through the war zone to Bocay, in solidarity, and begged our troupe to come. We deliberated and altered plans.

Mark marching through a war zone in Nicaragua.

About eighty of us traveled, first on some big utility vehicles, and then on foot, through the jungles. We saw bombed-out vehicles and often heard gunfire in the distance. We stopped along the way for a series of "actos," or interactions with the people, in the small towns. The towns were filled with women and children, as well as men who were too old to fight. These "actos" were quite the experience, and we heard some harrowing tales from the locals, listened to the concerns of the internationalists, and shared the gift that we could give them all: our performance.

As we neared Bocay, the women and children came out to meet us, and we walked in procession to the town square. We were surprised to see that some thousand Sandanista soldiers had also arrived and that there was to be a convening of the top generals. The Sandanistas had just routed the Contra army back across the border into Honduras. Again, we were invited to the "acto" and heard top generals speak. I was in another zone, looking out on the soldiers standing in formation on the square, shocked to see a bunch of young boys with machine guns and mortar rifles.

Sandanista soldiers celebrate a victory in Bocay, Nicaraga.

When we performed, I announced that we were "malabaristas por la paz," and as I looked out, I felt like Bob Hope entertaining the troops but for the wrong side. (Some of you may be too young to understand.) We pulled a perfect routine, no drops. Afterward, we went to the mash tent and did some interaction and performance for the wounded, and I had a chance to converse with the young soldiers. I was struck by a world where innocent people have to fight in wars that they do not really understand, against unknown enemies. Later, we went to Ben Linder's home and had a chance to handle his props, paying homage to a fallen juggler.

Bringing these memories home with me, and reflecting on them, I realized the truth in that old saying "Think globally, act locally." To be most effective, I needed to care for the people right here in my community. Starting in Hillsboro Village, and later working in other Nashville urban neighborhoods, I knew the key to bringing people back to the city was in creating a vibrancy that facilitated new business in order to inspire residential growth. Neighborhood commercial districts would be the draw that would be most impactful to the adjacent neighborhoods. I couldn't solve the problems of Nicaragua, but I could have a big impact in my hometown.

Betty Nixon, a councilwoman for District 18, had emerged as a Hillsboro Village champion, fighting to keep Vanderbilt University at bay and encouraging them to be good neighbors. Betty had helped the neighborhood create new relations with the university and encouraged them to stop their expansion. Vanderbilt cooperated and even started to police the area, making sure that students who lived in the quads and duplexes respected the neighborhood. District 18 included Belmont Hillsboro and Hillsboro West End and the quaint commercial district on Twenty-First Avenue South known as Hillsboro Village. I was a big fan of Betty Nixon, and when she ran for mayor, I campaigned for her. I still have "Betty Nixon for Mayor" stickers on my swinging clubs from the days I juggled to get out the vote.

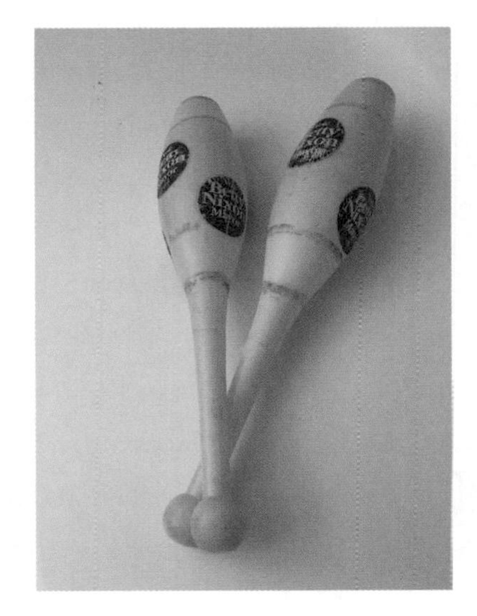

When Vanderbilt hired Jane Cleveland to improve neighborhood relations in Hillsboro Village, Jane and I, along with other neighbors, worked to jump-start the merchant's association to create a strong commercial core. A strong commercial district would draw others to this community. In addition, and to help the process get started, Joel and I invested in a few properties in Hillsboro Village, renovating them for our offices.

With the merchant's association in place, we formed a streetscape committee and worked to find funding to improve the sidewalks, the landscaping, the signage, and the art. As part of the committee, Jane and I had cohosted the first annual Hillsboro Village Neighborhood Tour and Halloween Festival to improve public awareness about the merchants and classic old homes in the neighborhoods and to showcase the community's "walkability." We invited everyone who liked the classic homes to tour the neighborhood and wrapped up the night with music, food, and a costume party in the middle of Hillsboro Village.

Focusing on the two neighborhoods on either side of Twenty-First Avenue, I learned that the home values on the east side, in the Belmont Hillsboro neighborhood, were 20 percent lower than on the opposite side of the road, in the Hillsboro West End neighborhood. I also learned that there was a perception that the homes were in worse condition as one moved east across the neighborhood. Perhaps they were at the time. If you crossed Belmont Boulevard, the values dropped another 20 percent.

Gene TeSelle was the champion of the Belmont Hillsboro neighborhood and worked to promote integration and to restrict encroachment of the commercial corridors into the district. Though the homes were wonderful, most needed lots of work, and many had been dissected into rental duplexes, triplexes, and quads. I was passionate about the neighborhood but had my work cut out for me each time I listed a home.

But as Hillsboro Village continued to improve, the neighborhoods became more attractive, and the pace of renovations of these classic homes—most built in the 1910-1940 era—accelerated. The values of the homes, which in the late 1980s were in the $60,000 to $110,000 range, began to rise. When Stewart Clifton became the metropolitan councilman for the neighborhoods, he put a conservation overlay on upper Music Row but allowed them to "legally" become commercial, which not only saved the historic studios but allowed the mom-and-pop shops to prosper. This buffered the neighborhood's north side and gave a nod to our music heritage and the many music professionals who had made their homes here. I was in the right place at the right time, and demand for my real estate assistance was strong. It was a lot of hard work in those early years, but I learned, partnered, and grew as a community builder, and people were beginning to take notice. My work in Hillsboro Village won me the coveted Betty Nixon award, and I was regularly voted the *Nashville Scene*'s Best Realtor.

Joel and I got involved with Bob Bernstein and invested with him in Bongo Java, which opened its first coffeehouse on Belmont Boulevard, another mini neighborhood commercial district with vast potential to emerge. A few years later, Bob opened a second, called Fido, in the old pet store in Hillsboro Village. The coffeehouse craze caught on slowly in Nashville, but it is now certain that coffeehouses are critical for connection and community. It's hard to fathom a world without a coffeehouse on every corner of every cool neighborhood, and Nashville now has quite a number of choices. It wasn't always that way.

Bob is very creative and comes up with all sorts of publicity ideas, but one in particular stands out from that time. When Bongo Java started baking cinnamon buns, one of his employees discovered a bun that looked like Mother Teresa's face. The PR release was picked up on the AP network, and the story circulated around the world. I happened to be in Miami when it hit and saw Bongo Java on the front page of the Miami Herald. Bob actually got a letter from Mother Teresa asking him not to use her name with the likeness, but nonetheless the Nun Bun was a hit. To this day, Bob has continued to use crazy marketing ideas to promote his growing business. "Just too weird to franchise" is his motto.

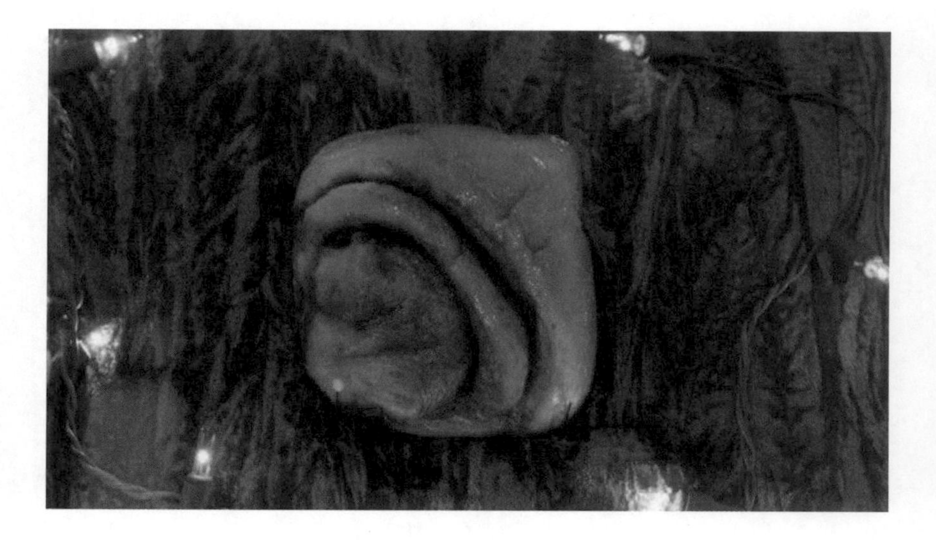

My early sales territory at Renaissance stopped at Belmont Boulevard but included Twelfth Avenue South, the next commercial corridor. I lived in this neighborhood, having purchased a 2,700-square-foot bungalow on Caruthers Avenue in 1986 for $73,000. I lived in the small side of the duplex and rented the big side to my tenants, Yusef Harris and Sizwe Herring. Interestingly, this move was a nuanced lesson in community building and politics. Yusef and Sizwe were black activists. Yusef was the founder of Alkebu-Lan Images, a bookstore on Jefferson Street. Sizwe went on to found the organization Earth Matters. We had a household engaged in civic activity, but the five homes next to mine were boarded up and vacant.

Later, I moved my young family to another home on Clayton, across the street from Sevier Park. I knew the area well and had done a significant survey of the commercial district. This was one of the places Joel and I did a lot of our night walks, looking for real estate deals and assessing the neighborhood. We picked up seven homes in the $40,000-$50,000 range near Twelfth Avenue and used them as rentals. We were aware that Twelfth Avenue South was a blight to the neighborhood and started thinking about an improvement strategy.

In 1994, Joel and I got into a discussion with Judy Steele, who was serving with us on the Hillsboro Village streetscape committee and working for the MDHA, about the current state of Twelfth Avenue South. We talked about the district's vacancy rate of over 50 percent; its crime rate, drug dealers, and prostitutes; and how we felt this was an impediment to the revitalization of the entire neighborhood. We wondered what we might do to stimulate growth there. Judy took our ideas back to Phil Ryan, who was a Hillsboro Village neighbor and activist, and at that time the executive director of the MDHA. Starting in 1994, our working group—the MDHA, the neighborhood, and 1221 Partners, which Joel and I started to focus on investments between Twelfth and Twenty-First—implemented an improvement plan for the sector from Ashwood Avenue to Clayton Avenue.

Phil Ryan and his team at the MDHA organized the existing merchants and held meetings to get their feedback about what was needed to improve the street. Merchant representatives from Becker's Bakery, Corner Music, 20th Century Christian Bookstore (now 21st Century Christian Bookstore), Mafiaoza's, Minor Jewelry, and the Islamic Center of Nashville, among others, were invited. The meetings were well attended, and we learned that the most important issues for all involved were safety, sidewalks, lights, and traffic calming. The merchants wanted to get the stream of commuters on this busy street to slow down and take notice.

In late 1994, 1221 Partners bought its first building at Twelfth Avenue and Paris, which we named the Paris Building. It was in fair condition, and we paid $150,000. I vividly remember having a closing celebration with our friends at the property. They all thought this was a crazy investment and that we must be out of our minds.

We did a study of all of the properties and decided to focus on the vacant ones. By our count, there were just fifty-one commercial properties. We felt that if we could influence renovation on a significant number of them, we could influence change. We purchased eleven properties over the next couple of years, ranging from $40,000 to $150,000. We had no interest in holding most of them, as it was our intention to generate more energy on the street. One of the buildings at Twelfth and Elmwood was an H.G. Hill owned property with a five-thousand-square-foot building that was in disrepair, situated on a couple of overgrown lots. We asked H.G. Hill to step up and be good stewards or to part with the property. They were heavily involved in a Hillsboro Village renovation at the time and said that they were having trouble mowing the overgrown lot at Twelfth because of the mattresses and used syringes, and thus agreed to sell. They sold to us for $130,000, with owner terms.

We attracted a number of new merchants. We flipped one building that we had contracted to Whitney Ferre for $1, and she started the Creative Fitness Center. We sold another to Monica Holmes, and she started the Clean Plate Club. After fully renovating several others, we sold them to owners/users. The Paris Building housed a pottery studio and offices upstairs for Andre Conte's nonprofit, You Have the Power. We renovated the former H.G. Hill building and found a home for Trim, a hair salon, and Laurel's Raw Bar. We bought a couple of buildings at Linden, which now house Serendipity and Art & Soul. Even as we worked to create a new identity for the area and to increase area business, it wasn't easy for the early tenants, and some surrendered and moved on.

We also strengthened our political connections, providing some space in the Linden building to a young man named Chris Ferrell for his Council-at-Large campaign. At twenty-five, this dynamic candidate took the race and the top vote. Later, when Chris and his wife, Molly, bought a home in the neighborhood, Chris dedicated time and energy to the cause. Chris likes to remind me of an early meeting with neighborhood leaders and of the moment when I suggested that we needed to change the brand of the neighborhood. "We should call it 12South," I said. Hmm, good idea.

1221 Partners took charge of the neighborhood marketing efforts and created the 12South Neighborhood Commercial District. We worked with the burgeoning merchants' association to promote the businesses. The MDHA helped rally some funds, and we created a streetscape committee. Gary Hawkins, of Hawkins Partners, led the master planning efforts for MDHA. The first phase was completed at a cost of $775,000, and funds included $168,000 from the infrastructure budget of Councilman Mansfield Douglas (the councilman that I roasted at a GNR event for Metro Council). Christine Kreyling, a writer for the Nashville Scene, said, "With 12South, MDHA has proven what the traffic engineers still largely ignore: that dollars spent turning streets into roads must be followed by more dollars spent turning pass-throughs back into places." This is something that traffic engineers and property owners are grappling with again today as the master plan contemplated to create walkability on 8th Avenue South in Melrose is being debated.

On June 18th, 1999, Mayor Phil Bredeson cut the ribbon dedicating the first phase. Ironically, the mayor's wife Andrea Conte leased office space with 1221 Partners in the Paris Building, our first purchase, and was a tenant with her nonprofit You Have the Power for seventeen years.

Phase 2, the rest of the street, was funded, at a cost of $2 million, during Mayor Purcell's administration. The early work had its impact, and over time the community has thrived. Today there are no vacancies on the street, and the merchants there are enjoying robust business. The issue is no longer about slowing the traffic to get people to stop and notice the businesses, but rather what to do with all the cars that stop and park. The merchants are well organized and have a bunch of promotional events each year, including the 12South Concert Series and the 12South Winter Warmer. The values of homes in the neighborhoods on each side of the street have increased dramatically, and I would argue that it is one of the more highly sought places to live in the city.

When Purcell became mayor in 1999, he called and asked me to serve on the Metropolitan Board of Equalization, which serves to compare and equalize property taxes. In essence, those of us on the board act as a liaison between people and businesses and the Assessor's Office. When he called, I initially said that I was busy and that furthermore I was concerned about compromising my business. I often, when listing and selling houses, had noted that the property assessment was consistently lower than the market value, and I did not want to be a "tax rat." Purcell, however, is persuasive, and he checked with Metro Legal and let me know that I did not have to rat out my customers. I accepted and served through Purcell's two terms.

Every year, people and businesses have an opportunity to challenge their assessment, and every four years all properties are reassessed. The board meets two times per year and hears these cases. First, I noted that there were a lot of residential hearings and that I was useful in the process, quickly able to analyze and help our board come to a decision. Second, I noted that there were a lot of elders coming before us, and that taxes were an important component in their cost of living. We were generally compassionate with these elders but also directed them to seek the tools available for tax relief. Fast-forward to 2017, a reassessment year after many years of significant increases in property values, and the current board will find that many who have long owned their urban homes are in need of support.

Many of my buyers at that time were coming from suburban neighborhoods. Years before, they had relocated from other cities and had, unfortunately, hooked up with corporate relocation agents and firms that directed most newcomers to the suburbs. These were folks who, after living near Nashville for a couple of years, had discovered the classic urban neighborhoods and preferred walkable communities over the commute they'd been sold. Some buyers came from out of town, looking for urban lofts—old converted warehouses they'd come to love in other cities with a vibrant core. Early on, I had to tell them that this kind of housing did not exist, but "How about a nice bungalow in Hillsboro Village?"

In addition to there being very little housing downtown, the zoning codes restricted the creation of mixed-use and residential projects. We had a strong central business district with a restrictive zoning code that had been in existence for fifty years. It had been created when our city's leaders wanted to get rid of residual housing downtown so that the business community could occupy and thrive. The problem with the code, however, was that this urban residential squeeze, coupled with urban flight, meant that retail commercial establishments could not survive, and they gradually left for the suburbs, too. This was not good for the business community. Other than the tourist traffic at the honky-tonks on Lower Broad, not much was happening after hours or on weekends. In the late 1990s, Nashville woke up and shifted policy so that that our city could again begin attracting residents and retail.

This zoning shift in the core led to the potential for increasing residential density. With codes in place that allowed for more height, developers utilized smaller land parcels to build up instead of out. In the core, and on major corridors, density is a good thing. For downtown Nashville, it created alternative uses for the eighty-four old buildings that were either vacant or semi-vacant. These old structures had no viable use at the time and had been vacant for years. It was too expensive to develop them into class A or B office structures. They were underutilized, had maintenance issues, and were generally blighted. Earlier downtown development efforts had, unfortunately, chosen to raze these structures, which was a shame, given that urban classics are important heritage buildings that define a city's character. Fortunately, the code changed in time to breathe new life into many of these old structures before they were destroyed.

During this time, my young company, Village, conducted a strategic planning process to better understand the multifamily residential market. With Nashville changing its code downtown, these higher-density projects would be apt to emerge. Looking at patterns in other cities, it was also likely that we'd begin to see residential density on some of our corridors.

In order to ready myself for this, I studied with urban sales teams in Chicago and Vancouver—two cities that were way ahead of us in the urbanization movement—and learned about projects and sales from some of the best. My favorite mentor, Bob Rennie, the "condo king" in Vancouver, who had sold something like $1.5 billion worth of condos the year that we spoke, gave me some good advice: beware of working with developers who are too proud of their project. The emerging vision allowed us to support the sale of multifamily and mixed-use residential developments while reusing the existing infrastructure, enhancing the value of our urban core, and creating walkable neighborhoods.

Our first sales project, named Row 8.9, for Eddie Latimer and Steve Neighbors of Affordable Housing Resources (AHR), was in Hope Gardens. AHR is a nonprofit organization whose mission is to create affordable housing and strong neighborhoods. We sold many of the twenty-nine residential units in-house, finding capable buyers for the affordable one- and two-bedroom townhomes located just across from Farmer's Market. I was impressed that people were willing to pay for this product in North Nashville and was intrigued by the emerging market.

As our multi-residential strategy advanced, Village and the City-Living Group, my personal sales team, began to market and sell some of the other projects that were emerging downtown. We sold the Lofts at the Exchange, Ambrose Lofts, Kress Lofts, and even some that were never built, such as the Utopia Lofts on Fourth Avenue, over Printer's Alley. The condo market downtown gained steam, and we sold Art Avenue Lofts, Church Street Lofts, District Lofts, and lofts at Fifth and Main.

We launched sales on these projects by creating a storyboard and worked to help folks through a purchase process by first showcasing the neighborhood and location and pointing out walkable highlights. We then discussed with them the possibilities of additional amenities, including swimming pools, rooftop decks, and fitness

▲
The Enclave
Advertising (2005-06)

Rolling Mill Hill
Advertising (2006-07), Initial Launch
▼

▲
Rolling Mill Hill
Promotional Flyer (2010), Reboot / 2nd Launch

Graphic design by Donna Huff, Solve

▲
Fifth & Main
Advertising (2006), Initial Launch

▲
Fifth & Main
Brochure & Advertising (mid-2011)
Reboot / 2nd Launch

▶
Fifth & Main
Advertising (early 2012)

centers. If the customer was still engaged, we dug into floor plans and unit amenities.

Ideally, we were able to create a sense of urgency and excitement. We generated a lot of signed contracts at our launch events. We were selling a new lifestyle, where people would meet and have their lives shifted and shaped by their experiences. We loved working with these people—the early pioneers in our city who would, over time, set the stage for Nashville's renaissance.

During that time, I liked to host bus tours to showcase the emerging market. I planned a big tour of the condo projects downtown, arranging two big buses to meet the hundred registered guests at the Bicentennial Mall. The market was obviously getting hot, and 250 people showed up. I didn't know what to do with this overwhelming response, so I yelled, "First come, first served! Get on the buses! The rest of you need to car pool!"

We went downtown, and I took people through a bunch of vacant buildings at the Kress, the Exchange, the Westview, and Utopia. Looking back, I realize I must have been immune to liability: I took all of those people up back stairwells and all over those decrepit old buildings without anyone suffering an injury.

Before any of these downtown mixed-use/residential lofts were created, there had been only ten owner-occupied units downtown, and back then I liked to joke that I would marry the first buyer to close on one of the emerging projects. Sherry Stewart was that buyer when she bought a condo at the Westview, and of course I kept my word! I later learned that she was on the bus the day of my tour.

While we were getting people excited about these new multi-residential communities, Village engaged with the Nashville Downtown Partnership (NDP). Started in 1994, the NDP is a private, nonprofit corporation whose core purpose is to make downtown Nashville the most compelling urban center in which to live, work, play, and invest in the Southeast. The NDP has become a leadership organization that focuses on business recruitment and retention, residential and retail development, public space management, access and transportation, and communications and marketing. The NDP was one of the early cheerleaders of urban living and continues to host a popular annual home tour. Village worked with them and showcased many lofts during this weekend event. Thousands of people attended. There was so much buzz that I decided to open an office downtown, at Third and Church, at the base of Church Street Lofts. I used this as the home for Village and the CityLiving Group for a number of years.

Multifamily residential projects were now emerging everywhere in Nashville. Back in Hillsboro Village, my team advanced our development sales portfolio with an in-fill condominium project of thirty-six units called the Glen. We sold Bristol on Broadway, the Enclave, Bristol West End, and others as the surge proceeded, and for the first time we were getting a taste of urban density. Solve, a partnership with Jenn Garrett, was born. Solve focused on marketing management, transaction management, and sales management for multifamily sales, and supported the CityLiving Group as we worked to reduce development risk and to sell out projects.

We then sold Icon and Velocity in the Gulch and Rhythm on Music Row. Now midtown and the Gulch were on the map. These were exciting times, and as we entered 2008 I had well over a thousand pending contracts in my name. I was at the top of the chart in the *Nashville Business Journal* for quite a few years as the lead residential agent in both volume and units. It was a whirlwind. We were presenting for the listings on projects left and right as more people tried their hand at development.

Fascinating and surprising evolutions happened as a result of revitalizing the core; people came together in a way they never had before. Perhaps a perfect example of this is the Nashville staple, hot chicken, which became emblematic of the cultural diversity and evolution of our city.

Hot chicken, primarily sold in what were our black neighborhoods for over seventy years, is suddenly the rave, not only in Nashville but in the kitchens of renowned chefs from New York City to Detroit. Said to have been conceived by a jilted woman seeking revenge against a known womanizer, Thornton Prince, the plan backfired when he tasted her extra spicy fried chicken. He loved it and took it to his brothers, who launched Prince's Chicken Shack.

In her newsletter, *The Bitter Southerner*, Rachel L. Martin notes that she, a native of Nashville, moved away in 2005 for graduate school, having never heard of hot chicken. When she started seeing articles about this "must try" southern food, she came back to what she describes as a new Nashville with hot chicken on her food bucket list and saw a city that was growing faster than developers could manage, historic neighborhoods being razed and renewed, and friends moving to neighborhoods that they'd avoided growing up.

She traces the story back to the Civil War, when Nashville became a very segregated city, when white neighborhoods and black neighborhoods shared very little public space. Fast-forward, and she writes about the invention of hot chicken and how segregation complicated the Chicken Shack's popularity, as Prince's needed a place to seat their white celebrity clientele without alienating their black customers. She then goes on to describe the evolution of hot chicken restaurants throughout Nashville, their impact on neighborhoods, and where we stand today. The story has some parallel to other pieces of the changing urban fabric given that many new hot chicken restaurants are being founded, many by young white men in popular gentrifying districts. This story was an example of what can happen cross culturally when you strengthen your core.

Mayor Purcell and his mother Mary leading the Hot Chicken Festival parade.

Mayor Bill Purcell deserves much of the credit for the current craze. Purcell, as mayor, was a frequent guest of Prince's, calling it his second office. He was looking for something important to the soul of our city as we were approaching our bicentennial and cited hot chicken as one of our indigenous foods that deserves celebration. He launched the Hot Chicken Festival in East Park in 2007. The festival has grown over the years, attracting over fifteen thousand guests in 2016. Purcell is passionate about hot chicken and encourages all of his friends (or enemies?) to indulge. Indeed, he's been calling on me and the Village Fund to sponsor the festival since its inception and always encourages me to try the hottest varieties.

Of course, as we concentrate on developing the core, new challenges come up. Affordable housing in the city was not an issue at the time we began this initiative, as property was relatively inexpensive. We were more concerned about absentee landlords and run-down, uninhabited properties than we were with gentrification. We wanted to populate underutilized neighborhood commercial districts and were not concerned about how the success of these businesses, along with parking issues, might impact neighborhoods.

As the city has heated up, I have come to realize that this big, positive change for some—those who have the money and resources to purchase property in these thriving neighborhoods—means that others, living on low incomes, can end up unable to pay even the increased property taxes. So, in order to help families and seniors "age in place" while maintaining social and community ties, I am devoting more time to looking for ways to mitigate the harmful aspects of shifting demographic and economics at the core and hope that government provides better tools for the elderly.

Despite the strengthening of our urban neighborhoods, the reality is that the United States remains a largely suburban nation.

The exodus to suburbs that resulted from the invention and proliferation of the automobile has created an enduring appeal. In America's largest metropolitan areas, suburbs account for 79 percent of the population. From 2000 to 2015, according to the ULI Terwilliger Center for Housing, suburban areas accounted for 91 percent of the US population growth. Of particular note, 76 percent of the minority populations in these metro areas live in the suburbs, as do 75 percent of young adults aged twenty-five to thirty-five. Nashville mirrors all of these trends, and it is thus important that those of us working to enhance core neighborhoods remember to think regionally as we tackle various issues.

With this in mind, how does this impact my work? Reflecting on that trip to war-torn Nicaragua, where two sides of the same community were in conflict, it starts with that initial belief that we have a responsibility to create a core that serves all and to do so with purpose and vision. It takes commitment to stay the course.

Daily, I strive to practice what I preach and deepen my workings within a one-mile radius. There was a time, however, in the late 1990s, when I was tempted to branch out (the suburbanization of Village?). I was considering something that I called the Village Referral Network and put together a business plan for an Internet-based referral system. This was my early version of what Zillow and others are doing today, but my project had a community component, with the Village Fund, and a strong urban-to-urban focus. I believed in the potential impact of the cultural creatives and felt that I could appeal to their sensibilities.

I attended the Social Venture Institute (an annual SVN entrepreneur training event) at Hollyhock in 1999 and presented my plan in front of the conference attendees and a panel of experts. The four panelists included Gary Hirshberg, of Stonyfield/Dannon renown, and a couple of venture capitalists from Silicon Valley.

As I finished my presentation, the attendees were buzzing in excitement, and Gary yelled "Lock the door!" The panel proceeded to give me feedback. They advised me to slim down my presentation to one page, move to Silicon Valley, and find someone who would back me with $10–15 million. One of the venture capitalists gave me a mock check for $1 million and asked me to contact him soon.

And, oh, they all recommended that I shut down my Nashville operations.

This was all very exciting, but it posed a dilemma. Village was growing nicely in Nashville, and I had a home, a family, and a lot of agents depending on our existence. While the allure of the shiny new venture was tempting, it was fraught with uncertainty. And, to be honest, I was concerned about Y2K and the impact it might have on the economy. So, I filed away the business plan and stayed the course. On December 31st, 1999, my then-wife and I hosted a party called "The Last Supper," inviting a couple of hundred guests for food, drink, and communion from 7–10 p.m. We sent them home or out to other parties early, because I did not want to be responsible for anyone's Y2K moment.

Though Y2K turned out to be an idle threat, six months later the dot-com bubble burst and many rising Internet business stars fell back to earth. I was grateful for my intuition and inaction, knowing that I would likely have been a casualty, given the short window from my idea to the dot-com crash. Now, many years later, I see some of the elements of the plan in action but remain satisfied with my body of work here at home.

It's tempting to abandon your own community, your core. Nashville's core had been abandoned in the urban flight of the 1960s and 1970s, but what we found when we focused our attention on it was that the core did not actually die—it was evolving. I had learned about equity and fairness and oppression in Nicaragua. This had sparked a passion to be part of Nashville's evolution, and for using the existing infrastructure to create a new way of living in cities.

It's a slow process. Developers may start making changes in a particular area, but it takes the community itself to truly decide what it will become. The one-mile radius metaphor describes the impact of concentrated work in a neighborhood. Here in Nashville, I've witnessed firsthand how the combination of community work, sales activity, political input, and development can activate and stimulate the evolution of neighborhoods and commercial districts and create a strong core that can reverberate outward.

Chapter 6

Skin in the Game

In your career, even more than for a brand, being safe is risky. The path to lifetime job security is to be remarkable.

—Seth Godin,
Purple Cow: Transform Your Business by Being Remarkable

AS NASHVILLE'S CORE was beginning to thrive, contractors were beginning to see new potential for some of its iconic structures. In the early 2000s, a group of contractors were considering the possibility of loft housing in the old Werthan complex, a four-hundred-thousand-square-foot, sprawling warehouse on ten acres in Germantown that had been vacant for years. They wanted my opinion on sales. We toured the building, which housed flocks of pigeons and plenty of flaking, lead-based paint, but which was also wonderful and open. You could walk each floor from one end to another with no obstruction.

The Old Mill, built in 1872 as a cotton mill, was a four-story, heavy-timber building with beautiful old beams, pockmarked original flooring, a central interior tower, and turret-like extensions framing each side. The remains of scales and pulley systems from the former factory were still intact. Adjacent was a second building, the New Mill, constructed in 1882. From 1928, these buildings had been home to the Werthan Bag Company and were now owned by a savvy gentleman by the name of Charles Jones.

Charles and his contractor friends were looking at various development concepts, including one in which each contractor took a floor of the Old Mill, joining forces to create a loft development. This plan was not really plausible, as banks were not predisposed to lend to this type of partnership, particularly in a big, unwieldy project that would require multiple phases.

That said, customers in Nashville were hungry for true loft spaces, and we knew that if we built it, they would come. People who had moved here from this type of housing in other cities, as well as local artists and musicians who needed studios, would buy these lofts, I believed, given that I had, with my urban focus, fielded so many inquiries through the years. I took a group of thirty of my Village agents through the building and asked them, "Can you sell it?" They insisted resoundingly, "Yes!" The idea was fun to imagine, but we realized that without a master architect and master developer detailing how to deal with major infrastructure, lead-based paint mitigation, financing, a homeowners association, and other details inherent in a development project, it would be tough to actualize. The original plan had too many flaws.

I hired Aaron White, a smart young man with business savvy but little development experience, to look at the project and advise me how to move forward. Aaron, who later became a partner in Core Development, returned and said, "Mark, I advise you not to do this project. It is too risky." He was right, of course, but I was adamant and said, "I hired you to tell me how to do it." He went back to the drawing board, and we came up with a workable plan. We laugh today about this interchange, and Aaron was integral to the project's ultimate success. We worked through the many challenges, took control of the project, and became the sole development team.

The Werthan Mills Loft project was the impetus for the creation of a sister company to Village, Core Development, a venture that began in 2003 as Village Development Services. While I had some development experience with homes and neighborhood commercial investments, I had never tackled a major project. My background in sales and marketing was an unusual gateway for a developer, given that most come from a background in finance, architecture, or construction. The possibility of becoming the developer of the old warehouse was daunting, but my understanding of loft demand in the marketplace, my group of urban-minded agents, my love for the old buildings, and my strong political and community contacts made me best suited to give it a go. The company was created to conceive, develop, and sell what would become the ambitious, five-phased, 342-unit Werthan Mills Lofts.

The plan, as it emerged, was to build out the infrastructure in the Old Mill and to develop Phase 1. We designed a single loaded corridor, giving each unit views facing downtown. The windows in the building were spaced such that each bay, which was the space from window to window, front to back, was four hundred square feet. We sold the units in bays, with the option to buy two, three, four, or more bays. We even sold multi-bayed, two-story loft units with various combos, such as three bays up, two bays down. Some of the bays, such as the ones on the first floor, had a loading dock, which would serve as an exterior porch for those units. The end units

got the turrets, which created a wonderful internal space. The top floor units had attic space, which we opened to spacious mezzanines. The lower floor had a great basement below, and we gave that space to the owner for future expansion. Eventually, we created twenty-three eclectic lofts in this phase.

These early days of Werthan Mills Lofts were a critical time for me. I had a lot vested in Village, and I was setting myself up for big bank debt and a potential bankruptcy. As the developer, I had to sign the bank note, pledging all assets in the event of a problem. The bank was requiring 80 percent presales before funding, and I was being asked to sign as the sole guarantor of a $6.5 million loan. This compares to a 30–40 percent presale requirement for Core Development condo projects today. I remember sitting on my front porch with my friend Hank Helton, letting him know that I had doubts. Hank listened and then promptly told me to buck up. "You are a developer now, Mark," he said. "You have to own it."

I did some soul searching, walking through the vast structure on my own, day and night. Day rambling and night walking again. One day I was in the building in one of the turrets and saw a Cooper's hawk sitting on a ledge. I realized that it must have entered to chase the pigeons but knew it would die if I didn't free it. I calmly approached it, reaching out with my bare hand to pick it up. It didn't panic, bite, or claw me. I opened the window with my other hand, reached out, and it flew away. I took this as a good sign, recalling my days with the Sioux elder, and found some peace with my decision.

The project got a kickstart when John Jameson came into the picture. John had come to Nashville when he discovered that he had a tumor in his lung. The diagnosis led to a treatment and surgery at Vanderbilt Medical, which had successfully cured his disease. In return, John had decided that he wanted to do something good for the city, and had discovered Werthan when flying in a helicopter. He approached me when he learned that we were involved in the project.

John was an heir to some money and let me know that he was a potential investor in our project. He had a vision for the development, and a keen business sense. We pulled him in to consult with us, and he, Aaron, and I worked to further develop the plan. John's version was to do the project in its entirety, and he pledged $20 million to take down the land. Our version was to do the project piecemeal and to find a bank to lend money for a small phase. I was enthused to have money at the table. It gave me fortitude.

As we deepened our connection, John revealed that his real name was John Vanderbilt Jameson and that he was heir to the wealthiest of the Vanderbilt line and had a trust with hundreds of millions of dollars. Unfortunately, the money was not readily available, and John was not clear on the timing. There were internal family issues, and what he'd already received was in an account in Germany. Ultimately, we decided to pursue the alternate strategy, which progressed. Over time, I consulted with John about other issues at Village, and he convinced me to hire him as a consultant with a title, managing director. He worked with me and my team on some of the key issues of the time, including new commission plans and a move to a big new building.

John's story was one of the most amazing I'd ever heard, and it was hard to believe. It was exciting that someone of money and influence had interest in my work. But as he gained influence, and others in the company got to know him, some on my board and in my company challenged his veracity. I defended John at first, then confronted him and asked for verification. The story was just not adding up. A group of agents at Village and Kelly Coty of Prix de Solde took matters in hand. They hired a PI to investigate and presented me with the findings.

Holy smokes! John was a convicted con man with a record in Omaha. Nothing of his story was true. His apparent con was to encourage an owner to go out on a limb, beyond his means, and then to swoop in when things got bad for an ownership position. John was immediately terminated, but there was unrepairable damage, and I lost several fine agents from my ranks.

I learned a lot from this experience. I was very sorry that I'd let money, or the promise of money, impede my vision. I hated that this had caused a rift in the culture of the company, and I worked hard to heal the wound. John's presence in the company and my receptiveness to his council had created divisions in my team at all levels, from my board to agents and staff, and I had been blinded. I made changes over time so that this would not happen again, but during his time at Village and Core, I had made several big moves—a new building, a new development—with John's "guidance," and there was no backing down. Additionally, I learned to rely on the wisdom and insight of known allies and to weigh incoming information with a dose of healthy skepticism. If it sounds too good to be true, perhaps it just isn't.

By the time we got to Phase 2 in 2004—twenty-seven units—we had more security. But it would still involve another bank loan, with my signature. The market was good, and we sold through and developed the project. I still wonder why these banks had faith in me, allowing me to be the sole signatory on these loans, and I thank Seth Butler, my banker who was there with me for the duration. Banks must take the fortitude and character of a developer and his team into consideration when they finance a project, because it took a while for us to create a good balance sheet. Phase 2 went well, and we soon completed our work in the original section of the Old Mill.

Phase 3, starting in 2005, included development of the wings that had been added to the Old Mill in the early 1900s and incorporated an original structure and outbuilding that was built in 1869. In this thirty-six-unit phase, we also created two courtyards for our residents and sold the original structure as a single unit, appropriately, to Bill Ivey, an American folklorist who was overseeing the National Endowment of the Arts at the time. Artists and musicians were sincerely attracted to the history, character, and eccentricity of Werthan Mills Lofts, and an art movement called Untitled started holding its annual event in the building, hanging art in the corridors and in the finished lofts. I remember walking through the building and into the units at this event, with some 1,500 other guests, and remarking how beautiful the homes had become with all of the additional artistic input from our residents.

One night about this time, and early in my courtship with Sherry, I drove her to Werthan Mills Lofts to show her my "work." In truth, I was just showing off and hopped out of the car next to the water tower. I've always liked to climb and for some reason looked up and saw a way to shimmy to the ladder. I hadn't climbed a water tower since my youth, so why not now, after a couple of drinks? When I was a kid, in Florida, I climbed the tallest palm trees. Later, I free-climbed cliffs and "ran" mountains, which is a term for running breakneck speed, off trail, down the mountain. I forgot myself for a moment.

I made it to the ladder and slowly worked my way up, testing the rungs at every level. Sherry is afraid of heights and admonished me to come down. I guess that spurred me on, and I must admit my legs were a bit shaky at the halfway point. Sherry now says, "I didn't know him that well yet, and he'd taken the car keys, or I'd have driven away. All I could think of is, "What am I going to say when Mark Deutschmann is splattered on the pavement?" I made it topside and enjoyed some of the most amazing bird's-eye views of Werthan and the city. Sherry didn't talk to me much on the way back home. Beyond showing off, though, I was proud of what I'd done and happy to have shared it with her.

In 2006 we continued to build Werthan Mills Lofts with beauty and community in mind and started work on the New Mill. At a cost of $28 million, the beginning of Phase 4 was a big deal, and this time John was out of the picture. My development team knew that we needed to create a large concrete parking structure and complete some of the amenities conceived in the master plan. We decided to finance 120 units, starting at the far end of the building, on Taylor Street. This phase included a lot of demolition and lead-based paint abatement, which required additional financing assistance. We approached the MDHA, which awarded $2 million in tax increment financing (TIF) to the project in exchange for an agreement by our development team to sell a minimum of 20 percent of the project to people who earned less than 80 percent of Nashville's median income. This was supported by Mayor Purcell, who recognized the need to address affordability as Nashville redeveloped neighborhoods in the core.

We built the planned 120 units, including sixteen new loft units over the parking garage, added a fifty-meter saltwater pool and the largest green roof in Nashville, and enhanced the project with an outdoor area complete with grills and a bocce court. We saved some concrete structures that had served as shells for sections that had been demolished, which added to the artistic flair. This phase also included a building addition from the 1940s, which had beautiful, enormous windows that had, over time, been bricked in. We opened these and added big garage bays so that the residents could be exposed to nature.

By the time Phase 5, also in the New Mill, was starting in 2010, we were in recession, and no one was lending for condominiums anymore. We decided to finance the project as a rental and were able to secure another $700,000 from the US Department of Housing and Urban Development (HUD) for lead-based paint abatement and demolition. We did this in exchange for some additional affordability for our rental tenants, primarily for people who made less than 60 percent of the median income in Nashville. We added a second swimming pool, located near the iconic water tower, a fitness center, and a yoga room. An outbuilding, the original boiler building on Taylor Street, was developed, and our tenant Rolf and Daughters

created an amazing restaurant that was quickly listed nationally in the top five by *Bon Appétit*. The development of Werthan Mills Lofts spanned twelve years, a major recession, and the ensuing financial crunch. The fifth and final phase was completed in 2012. Units were leased for a couple of years before the final sales push, which culminated in 2015.

This project is a perfect example of the potential for impact in a one-mile radius. The development of this large, iconic structure in the back corner of Germantown became an anchor for neighborhood investment and transformation. Over time the area's resurgence spread into neighboring Salemtown and in Germantown, toward the Cumberland River. Increased residential density attracted new restaurants and services, and other key investors entered the market, developing a number of large apartment buildings. In 2014, the area received another jolt with the addition of the Nashville Sounds, now playing AAA ball at First Tennessee Park. The ballpark, inside Jefferson Street, has itself spurred another wave of development. The city now has an exciting new mixed-use neighborhood next to the Bicentennial Mall, and Germantown is connected to downtown and the river. Due to this catalytic impact, and because of the creative adaptive reuse of a historic structure, Werthan Mills Lofts won the Excellence in Development Award from the Nashville chapter of ULI in 2014.

I am proud that sixty-three of the ninety-eight units sold were very affordable, allowing workforce and artist households to buy into the urban core. This is a case where TIF worked and why I believe that it should get broader use as our city aims to densify our corridors. With TIF, the city trades future property taxes from a project to create a loan for the developer, who in turn can do things that otherwise would not make financial sense or even be bankable. The developer obtains the TIF loan and is responsible for the success of the project, which will repay the loan; the city pledges future property taxes to fund the repayment, which ends when the TIF loan is paid in full. Results of the appropriate application of TIF can include affordable housing, artist and maker lofts, community rooms, and pocket parks. These assets can shape a vision for community, enhance the quality of a development, and create the amenities and homes needed in our urban neighborhoods, on our corridors, and for our city's workforce.

In 2005, as Phase 3 at Werthan Mills Lofts was underway, we'd gotten involved in a separate condominium project of forty-seven units on downtown Church Street at Printer's Alley, known as The Lofts at the Exchange. This was to be one of the first condominium projects downtown and the first of four that Core Development developed in the mid-2000s. The MDHA approached Core about a couple of buildings that were in danger of being demolished for parking and asked if we would consider a development. TIF was available as a development tool in downtown at the time, given the urban blight. As the Nashville Civic Design Center (NCDC) had noted, eighty-four buildings were mostly or totally vacant. The shift in the zoning code from the late 1990s now allowed for the conversion of some of these buildings to mixed use and for more residential loft space.

Core Development, with Aaron White and Hunter Connelly now my equal partners, worked with the MDHA to buy the buildings from the owner. One of the buildings, built in the late 1800s and located on Printer's Alley, was the Banner Publishing building, which was sadly burned out on the upper floors. The other, a 1950s building, had been built after the original building had burned down. Our architect, Ron Gobbell, worked with us to design the building as one project, with forty-seven units. We again worked with Solomon Builders, our construction partner on Werthan Mills Lofts.

It was fun to see the project come to life. In 2006, Core Development moved down the street to Third, buying and retrofitting three more late-1800s structures and creating Church Street Lofts. This was the conversion of an office building housing a law practice. The partners were looking for an exit strategy, and Core Development shifted the use to residential lofts. Village, the CityLiving Team, and Core Development anchored the commercial corner in this project for several years. We partnered with the Downtown Partnership, with the NCDC, and with GfN to address quality-of-life issues in the changing urban core. Meanwhile other, bigger condo developers had entered the mix, and the 305-unit, thirty-one-story Viridian was built near our projects on Church Street. Again, investment in historic structures within Nashville's urban core attracted even more investment.

At this time, the area around Fifth Avenue, known as the Arts District because of its relation to the Tennessee Performing Arts Center, the Arcade, and the Bridgestone Arena, had many underutilized structures. Core Development entered into an agreement to develop the Kress Lofts in 2005, after an original developer released the reins. Core turned a vacant, former five-and-dime into thirty-two true lofts and an art gallery. Then, in 2007, working with the neighbor for air rights, we bought the building two doors down, opened up the middle for a courtyard, and developed Art Avenue Lofts, another project of thirty-two lofts and another art gallery. Both downtown galleries are thriving today.

It is interesting to note that Fifth Avenue, and the Kress Lofts, is where the Nashville sit-ins originated. These were like the bus boycott that my Uncle Bob and Aunt Jeanie Graetz were involved in down in Montgomery, among the earliest nonviolent direct action campaigns in the South. This movement to desegregate Nashville's downtown lunch counters was led by the Reverend James Lawson, a devoted student of the Gandhian philosophy of direct nonviolent protest to show the hypocrisy of the segregated system. The protestors, mostly African American students from Fisk University, Baptist Theological Seminary, and Tennessee State University, convened at the Arcade on Fifth Avenue on February 15, 1960, and entered the diners at Woolworth's, McClellan's, and Kress, making small purchases and occupying the seats and the counters. The movement lasted throughout the spring, and the students suffered physical and verbal abuse, arrests, fines, and incarceration but held steadfast. Diane Nash and John Lewis, both students as Fisk University, emerged as major leaders, and the sit-ins resulted in a historic settlement. On May 10, the downtown stores opened their lunch counters to black customers for the first time, who were served without incident. With this agreement, Nashville became the first southern city to desegregate all public facilities. The sit-in movement served as a model for future demonstrations against segregated accommodations, unfair employment practices, and other examples of institutionalized segregation.

The central business district in Nashville today has enjoyed a significant shift toward renewed urban livability, and I've witnessed how Core Development's early residential projects—and other developments—have helped drive what is now an eighteen-hour city. With better policy and updated codes, with intention and investment, and with the hard work of many visionaries, our city has again embraced its core. For example, the area at Fifth and Church, at St. Cloud Corner, has changed dramatically from the days in the late 1980s when I first arrived in town and went to work at Joel's office. At that time, there were few if any residences. Today most of the vacant buildings have been retrofitted for residential, mixed-use, and even boutique hotels, one project at a time and over many years. In fact, noted restaurateur Tom Morales will soon open Woolworth on 5th, complete with a diner-style counter tops not unlike what was there in the sit-ins. The food served at the restaurant will draw from many of the cultural traditions that have shaped Nashville, with a focus on the ways African American history and culture influence society. The increased residential density now makes it easier to provide other services, including restaurants geared for residents and better retail options for all. When people live, work, and play in a compact area, lots of good things happen.

As Core Development projects progressed, Village was also growing up. From our humble beginnings with three agents in Hillsboro Village, we had penetrated urban markets across the city and grown to a team of more than a hundred agents. Perhaps for some agents it began with their attraction to our purple signs, the three stylized houses and swoosh of our logo, but for most it was much more. Many were attracted to the firm because of our culture, because we really were a village of professionals sharing a common vision, and because of the diversity in our ranks. Others saw the promise of being on a team in the heady multi-residential sales era that we were experiencing. And still others felt the excitement of what we were doing in communities, in our old ring neighborhoods, in midtown, and now in downtown.

But everyone who joined our team believed that we were doing something good for the city, supporting urban renewal, the Village Fund, and responsible development with Core and our many development partners. They were attracted to Village's growing presence and success but also our mission. I in turn began realizing that many of our agents had set down their own roots, successfully engaged with their own unique selling proposition, and were influencing a wider and wider community of buyers and sellers with their work. Though they might not use "one-mile radius" to describe their work, I sensed that it was now happening multifold. I felt that the old adage "It takes a village" was now our reality.

I, too, was growing up. I had a lot of skin in the game and was fully committed to our city. With some of the changes at the helm after the John Jameson era, I decided to let go of the brokerage, hiring Bobbie Noreen to be the managing broker. I was finally shedding what I could only call the "imposter syndrome," that nagging feeling that I did not belong in the leadership role. The syndrome is a concept describing high-achieving individuals who are marked by an inability to internalize their accomplishments and a persistent fear of being exposed as a fraud. It is actually common in entrepreneurial CEOs, who often grow beyond their ability to manage, and is most common in high-achieving women. For me it traced back to "not being good enough," one of my less admirable traits from childhood that continued to persist in its hold on me.

Giving up the brokerage, I was able to bring more focus to the business, had many fewer direct reports, especially now that the agents were taking their contract and client issues to Bobbie. Over time, we would grow the broker team, and Bobbie would need even more support in her expanding role. For now, she was much better suited for the role than I. I was free to spend more time studying the business of our companies, analyzing their KPIs (key performance indicators), and continuously developing our mission and vision. I also retained a sales team I could work with, the CityLiving Group, as I felt and still feel that it is important to have a pulse on the market, and because I generally just enjoy sales, something that I know I am good at. I was growing into my skin, taking the role of CEO by the horns, and finally felt right in my role. I would not abdicate the throne again!

Mark and Bobbie Noreen show off a Village listing.

This perspective allowed us to again think about strategic expansion. Our multi-residential sales skill set was relatively unique. We were involved with many projects, including many that Core was developing. We had learned about presales, project marketing, development hurdles, and risk management and by now had worked with both new build and adaptive reuse projects. One of our developer partners from Houston had launched a new project in Charleston, Bee Street Lofts, which we were hired to sell. Other developers, some local and some out of our market, had hired Solve to manage transaction, marketing, and sales management for other sales teams. Our logic was that if we could market this skill set to land developments in other cities, we could then leverage the sale, using the pending sales commissions to launch Village in that market. We looked for progressive cities that were accessible by Southwest Airlines without a layover and considered the opportunities.

It was an exciting time for the companies and for me.

With projects running smoothly downtown, Core Development then began to eye midtown, specifically a series of edge communities that would benefit from residential cottages. Starting in 2008 with West End Station in Sylvan Park on a five-acre parcel on the railroad tracks, we developed a cottage community of forty-five homes. We moved from there in 2009 to Gale Park, at the edge of Melrose and the commercial district, with a seventy-nine-home community. Core Development continued with a couple of other cottage series projects as the recession progressed, initiating the Chesterfield in 2012, consisting of forty-three homes in the Hillsboro Village neighborhood, and Richland Station in 2013, a forty-home community at the back edge of Sylvan Park at Charlotte Avenue and Fifty-Fourth. Each of these projects has acted as a stimulus to the adjacent neighborhoods and neighborhood commercial districts.

Core Development also changed course and, in 2012, bought out Aaron and Hunter so that Core's mission could include the development of sustainable for sale housing, with attainable price points, in our community. Aaron and Hunter started a new company, Evergreen, with an initial primary focus on rental development. As it goes, the separation was graceful, and all parties got the best of what they needed in the transition. Core Development retained the right to buy the last phase of Werthan Mills Lofts (Phase 5) from our partnership, and the right to several developments in the works, and traded interest in some of the apartment assets that we'd developed. I again became the president of Core. I am ever grateful to Aaron and Hunter for their impact and partnership in those formative years.

We realized too late in the project at Werthan Mills Lofts that we could have gotten a Leadership in Energy and Environmental Design (LEED) certification, which is today "the gold standard" in environmentally conscious and sustainable development. Given that we were recycling a massive old building that had fallen into economic obsolescence, that we were located on a major thoroughfare, that we were within walking distance of the city, and that we were reusing floors, beams, rafters, and brick, we could have scored a lot of LEED points. We didn't understand this fully at the time and could have worked harder to achieve a LEED rating. I still feel proud of the project and know that it was a "green" effort from start to finish.

What's fantastic about this kind of redevelopment is that the re-urbanization of Nashville and other American cities has profound "green" implications. This may sound counterintuitive given that population growth surely means more energy, but density in the urban core uses far less energy per person than the sprawling suburbs do.

Multifamily residential property, for instance, even in an old converted warehouse such as the Werthan Mills Lofts, is far more efficient than a bunch of single-family homes. The National Trust study from 2015 says that the most sustainable building is one that is renovated. Adaptive reuse involves less waste of materials and less need for new building materials like drywall, plaster, and concrete, which are highly energy and carbon intensive, even with the most sustainable production methodologies. It is getting progressively easier to make historic buildings more energy efficient. It is now much easier to obtain energy-efficient windows that can be inserted into a historic façade.

Residents of this type of housing have different social patterns, which often reduce the need for multiple cars and long commutes. The creation of vibrant neighborhood commercial districts in the urban core is much more efficient than the suburban alternative, where nothing can be reached without a drive. A comparison of Barcelona in Spain to Atlanta, each with roughly the same population, shows that Atlanta is taking up 26.5 times the space. Atlanta has a problem with cars, while Barcelona has virtually no problem with cars. Noted architect Lord Richard Rogers notes that compact cities—cities that have mixed living, working, and leisure, that are connected through transport and infrastructure, that have good public space, and that are well designed—these cities are already here. Some cities are doing it poorly, but some are doing it well.

The vision of an energy-efficient community is achievable via community-oriented development. In many places, it is already here and primed for continued community input. Starting with that massive project at Werthan Mills Lofts, we hope that we can continue to do it well with development projects that shape our city. What I have learned is that belief in this vision, even with the many unknown variables, can be good for communities and businesses. Still, a project such as that is one of those huge risks we take in business from time to time that we can't know the outcome of. We can only trust our intuition and follow our inner values and do a little hoping and praying. If you embark on such a feat, watch out for wooden nickels and con men!

Chapter 7

Rising through the Recession

Today is the first day of the rest of your life; do today what you want to be for the rest of your life.

—Unknown

SHERRY AND I married in May of 2008, just as the recession was beginning to show its true colors. Perhaps with recession in mind, but more likely because we'd both been married before, we chose to elope. We decided to have an elopement party at one of our favorite restaurants. We invited a hundred or so of our closest friends and family, greeted each of them with a drink at the door, and asked them to enjoy the party. After everyone had arrived, Sherry and I climbed up on the central hearth and welcomed our guests, who were waiting for us to disclose where we were going to elope. Someone yelled out, "Why don't you just get married?" We looked at each other and said, "This is quite a good idea." We invited our friend Stephen Mansfield to come forward and minister the service.

My mother, Suzanne Graetz Deutschmann, and my Aunt Jeannie Graetz react to the big news!

We had only told a couple of people about our plan, including our photographer. We asked him to be alert and to focus his shots on the crowd as they heard our big surprise. He got some great shots of jaws dropping as our friends and family realized they'd been duped. A spontaneous wedding is a beautiful thing and relieves many who might otherwise be stressed. The next morning, we took off for a honeymoon in Nova Scotia. A nice elopement party/wedding is a good cure for the recession blues.

During our short engagement, I had given Sherry a copy of my personal balance sheet. Sherry's company, LetterLogic, which prints and mails patient statements for hospitals and physicians' groups, is recession resistant, but my businesses, Village and Core Development, were right in the wheelhouse of the impending recession, and I had personal bank guarantees on three big projects. To her credit, I guess, she never looked at the numbers, and least not until later. She now says, "You never told me that you had so much debt!" Ah, but I did have so much debt, as did so many other developers in Nashville at that time.

When the Great Recession came to Nashville beginning in late 2008, the city's urban revitalization was in full swing. I told everyone that we were far from being overbuilt, we just needed to keep building toward a future of livable neighborhoods that extended to the core. I avoided reporters who wanted to spread bad news. But regardless of my efforts against the tide, the recession swept in. Condos in particular were stigmatized across the country. The overbuilding of condominiums in cities such as Atlanta, Las Vegas, and Miami were prominent in the news, and the local newspapers cast doubt on the viability of Nashville's urban market. Though not overbuilt, Nashville was caught up in the economic fallout, and many local projects failed.

With our focus on multi-residential sales, Village had "sold" a number of projects that were in preconstruction or under construction. I personally had over 1,500 pending condo contracts when 2008 rolled around. We had been riding high on our success and had dozens of projects in the works, optimistic that Nashville was ready to explode. We certainly did not anticipate being so thoroughly knocked off track. There was a collective sense of pending doom, and pessimists and the media both stirred the pot.

As the recession hit, the momentum quickly shifted. Fueled by a financial crisis involving mortgage derivatives, the recession instantly dried up financing for condo buyers. Bank terms changed. Many people could no longer qualify and were forced to default. Other buyers were just scared and refused to close. It turned into a vicious cycle, and many projects, such as Velocity, the West End, and Terrazzo, were hard hit and defaulted on construction loans.

Projects that we had sold, even with 90 percent presales, such as Rolling Mill Hill and Fifth and Main, were over budget and therefore out of time, and banks forced them into bankruptcy. Many other projects that we had sold later in the cycle lost construction financing and were never started. Developers who had deep pockets would fare better than others, but many developers had paid too much for properties for projects that now did not work and defaulted on acquisition financing. These properties went back to the bank. Village had spent lots of marketing money to achieve presales for these projects, and without closings this money was lost.

The collapse of our project at Rolling Mill Hill was particularly difficult and insightful. The MDHA, under the leadership of Phil Ryan, was the master developer of that thirty-four-acre site. With support for the development from Mayor Purcell, this parcel, above the city and at the highest point downtown, was promoted as a mixed-use community for Nashville's creative class, spurring the revival of a once-neglected section of our city. The site included the six red-brick trolley barns, beautiful old buildings with high ceilings of exposed wood and bowed trusses, and the beautiful and vacant old buildings that in the 1920s became the campus of the city's general hospital. The hilltop property was named from its original use as a processing terminal for wheat, corn, and timber, which went through the roller mills to the steamboats.

The MDHA had issued an RFP (request for proposal) for a number of parcels on the site, including the parcels that housed three of the existing structures. A company named Direct Development, based out of Wisconsin, won the RFP to become the developer on this parcel, and they had listed the project with Village. Their plan, as it evolved, was to renovate the three buildings and to build one new building to create about a hundred residential units in a first phase, retaining another portion for a new building in Phase 2. Working with their plans, Village created a sales center, preselling the necessary units for Direct Development to obtain a bank loan with Bank of America.

Village sales center at Rolling Mill Hill.

The three old buildings and this section of the site, which included the general hospital, the psychiatric ward, and the morgue for the city, had some bad residual energy. I'd even had a difficult personal experience in these buildings when my first wife's brother was murdered in the mid 1990s; I'd identified the body in the old Art Deco building. I was not the only one who sensed negative energy in and around the property. It was palpable.

I consulted friends, who recommended a number of site blessings. Kirby Shelstad, or "Grandpa Kirby" per my daughter Chelsea, practices Tibetan Buddhism, and he worked with senior monks to bless the site. These Buddhists engage in many cleansing rituals as part of their spiritual practice and have a special blessing to orient dwellings and other structures in an auspicious manner. Kirby and his wife, Sandy, performed what is called a Fire Puja and Dharmapala prayers and offerings, which is a purification ceremony that pays back karmic debt, purifies past negative actions, and creates conducive atmosphere. Additionally, he worked with the monks in India, who did similar ceremonies, as well as offering 108 butter lamps for purification and creating good circumstances.

I also invited musician friends to the site for some chanting and ritual, which included a resounding rendition led by Tom Kimmel of "Amazing Grace" in the old power stack. What was to be a third building on the site renovated to condos was crushed in construction, but the old stack still stands today. I also had an old-fashioned Baptist preacher come to the site for prayers and hedged my bets and had more prayers and blessings when Mayor Purcell and incoming Mayor Dean participated in the launch ceremonies.

We put a lot of energy and money into the project. Village paid for marketing costs and spent $300,000 to create successful sales and sold ninety units at an average of $305 per square foot. We were super excited about this site, which offers some of the best views of the city and the river, walkable access to downtown, and a mix of units with classic historic interiors, and sleek, modern units. Unfortunately, and even with rituals, prayers, songs, and my efforts to improve the feng shui, the project collapsed with the economy, and Rolling Mill Hill went back to the bank. It was a tough time for these developers and for Village.

Mayor Purcell talks about his vision for Rolling Mill Hill at the launch ceremony.

Bank of America foreclosed on the property. We had sold the approximately eighty thousand square feet of residential real estate for $24 million, and it sold in foreclosure to John Tirrell and his investment group for just under $8 million. I contacted John, a great guy, and we talked about the possibility, even in this recession, of a condo exit. I let him know that I had a bunch of buyers who were willing to close and that if he could offer condos at $200 per square foot, or $16 million for the project, I could sell all of the units easily. He gave it some thought but shared with me that his investment group was only familiar with apartments, not with condos. He finished the construction, leased it up, and sold the apartment project the next year for $11.5 million—a tidy profit. I still comment, with a smile when I see him, that he left money on the table.

Post-recession, the community has thrived, with the new Ryman Lofts for artists, Nance Place for workforce housing, and mixed-use projects with hundreds of apartments built by John Tirrell and his team. The area is undergoing a significant transformation, and the original vision is being realized. The trolley barns have been refurbished by Bert Matthews, and Hermitage Avenue is set to be a thriving neighborhood commercial district that will serve both the Rolling Mill Hill and Rutledge Hill neighborhoods. I hope that everyone benefits from the rituals and site blessings.

We nurtured the remaining condo sales from all projects and closed what we could. I estimate that I closed only 400 to 500 of my pending contracts, reducing commissions on many to get them closed. We worked with developers, for instance, at Icon in the Gulch, where we had presold 400 of the 420 units and closed as many as we could. We continued to sell that project at reduced prices over the next few years, managing to move 70 to 80 units a year.

As recession became a probability, Village downshifted from our prior sky-is-the-limit point of view. We began to tighten our belt. In September 2008, the stock market dropped 777 points, and the real estate market came to a screeching halt. We were planning 2009 budgets and aggressively cut anything that was not making money. In early 2009 we shut down a title company we had started, closed our offices downtown and in midtown on Church, and brought most of our people and resources back to our corporate offices at 2206 Twenty-First Avenue South. I remembered my lessons from previous involvement in Sun Tui, the undercapitalized, failed futon business, and conserved resources. It was a time to circle the wagons.

The recession was severe, and real estate took it on the chin, but Nashville was surprisingly resilient. The city was less overbuilt than other US cities and had a more balanced economy than most. We had stability with health care revenue and jobs and had entrepreneurial growth. In Nashville, prices fell, on average, only 13 percent in our metro area. In some walkable urban neighborhoods, such as Hillsboro Village, the price per square foot did not fall at all, though sales slowed. The development community was still hit hard, particularly when a developer was overextended. Big national banks were not forgiving and treated local developers like others in harder-hit regions. Condo developers and suburban developers with large tracts of land were among those most severely affected. Some developers never recovered.

As for me, the only way I could ever get things done, and to grapple with feelings of uncertainty and financial risk, was by creating goals and writing lists. As the recession came crashing down, I was having my forty-ninth birthday, which drove my goal setting to a new level. With nearly fifty years under my belt, I was looking at what I had achieved. I could see that there were some things that needed balancing and plenty of things that I still wanted to do. I did not want to let myself get caught up in a doomsday mentality.

Remembering that "today is the first day of the rest of your life; do today what you want to be for the rest of your life," I started a list, which I called fifty by fifty. I just started listing all of the things that I wanted to do before I turned fifty. I listed business goals, sales goals, Village Fund goals, goals that I could accomplish to support my wife and family, health and wellness goals, hobby goals, and so on. Some people call it a bucket list.

Before long, I had over a hundred goals on that list. Some were one-timers, such as "Travel to Europe with Sherry." Others were career based, such as "Sell sixty homes with Newell." Some were pie in the sky, such as "Take a submarine to the deep ocean trench," but I figured what the heck, I should have a few life goals on the list. Realizing I always do better when something is on a to-do list, I included all of the things I liked to do but seemed to always put aside for "more important" things. I include things like juggling, kayaking, bird watching, star gazing, and other things that give me personal fulfillment. My wife, who watched me put this list together, affectionately called me a freak, and friends who have witnessed my list making have affectionately agreed.

I figured that if I had over a hundred goals on my list, then surely I could get fifty of them done, chalk the year up as a success, and therefore feel good about my life and myself, even in a recession. And I thought I would likely accomplish some things across many categories, even if I didn't hit the numeric goals that I had set. I might only travel to British Columbia two times, though the stated goal was three, or I might only juggle twenty times, though I had set out to juggle twenty-five times. At least I'd be touching many aspects of my life that I find enjoyable. Many items on my list have to do with health, and truthfully I would not be as healthy or as disciplined with health initiatives without the reminder of a list. I believe that I exercise more, have less stress, and even weigh less because I am trying to achieve these self-manufactured goals.

I did, in fact, hit my fifty by fifty, and celebrated my accomplishment with another list. I decided to try again the next year and upped the ante, now setting an elevated goal, fifty-one by fifty-one. I looked back at the first list, saw where I'd had success, noted where I'd fallen short, and adjusted accordingly. I knew that this kind of list writing, and cumulative successes, had a positive effect on my psyche, and I began to think more about why. Now, after many years, I realize that this is a pretty extreme approach to tracking one's life, even during the crazy years of the recession, and I largely kept it to myself. But I decided to share it with Joel and his wife, Dana Bass Solomon, reading my current list to them on a recent visit, perhaps in an attempt to better understand the list's power in my life.

Joel, who you remember was on that remote island when I shipwrecked, is married to Dana, who has been the executive director of

Hollyhock for seventeen years. When I first landed at Hollyhock in 1983, a year after my boat caught on fire, the organization was just two years into its existence. During the recession, Hollyhock went through a remarkable transformation, becoming a nonprofit. We had worked together to turn shareholders into "share givers," and we all donated shares in what had been a for-profit in order to allow the legacy to flourish. When I gave Joel and Dana my list, Hollyhock had blossomed into Canada's unparalleled lifelong learning and leadership institute, there to inspire, nourish, and support people who are making the world better. There were no two people better suited to understand what list making meant to me and what it might mean to others. I've now enjoyed a long history with the organization and have served on the board for ten-plus years.

My friends, listening to my long list, were incredulous and could hardly imagine that one could conjure success and fulfillment in this way. Joel and Dana suggested that I share my list as an inspiration. And so I will. Here is a sample of my most recent list (I have removed a few very personal goals from the list, but you'll get the point) and a few goals from past lists.

+ = ***completed successfully***

+ President Greenways for Nashville

+ Chair of Mission Advance ULI

Chair elect for Greenways Commission

+ Surpass $1.5 million Village Fund

+ Retrofit 5 metro schools with HES

+ Retrofit 5 nonprofits with HES

+ Browns Creek plan complete

+ 440 Greenway work underway

+ $5 million for greenways in 2016 capital budget

+ Browns Creek Greenway approved

+ Megan Berry elected mayor

+ Colby Sledge elected District 17

+ Six10 sold out and closed

+ Twelve60 90 percent sold

+ Gentry sold and closed

+ Joule 20 vertical

+ East Greenway Park vertical

+ Herron under construction

+ Herron 50 percent sold

+ Bailey under construction

+ 7th and Taylor under construction

+ CityLights under construction

Trinity/Ellington SP complete

+ Secure three outside condo projects

+ Core/Village/Village parent split into 3 companies

+ Recruit to 300 agents

+ $80 million month at Village

+ Jason Pantana returns to Village

+ LetterLogic sales to $40m

+ Finish book

20 book presentations

+ 10 speeches

50 lessons Duolingo German

Learn to make ten new drinks

+ One life goal

+ 25 sessions 500 throws 5 balls juggling

+ 25 juggling sessions

+ 20 rounds of 9 holes golf

10 rounds of 18 holes golf

Bogie round

+ Paddle 5 rivers

+ 100 kayak rolls

+ Kayak adventure

+ 3 Joel visits

+ 3 international trips with Sherry

+ Visit 5 American cities

+ Buy property Cortes Island

+ 25 massages

+ 25 wins expert Scrabble

+ 15 crosswords with <10 letters missed

+ Read 50 magazines

+ Read 20 books

+ ID 50 birds

+ 5 new birds to life list

250 birding life list

+ ID 25 constellations

+ ID 5 new constellations

+ Weigh in under 169 100 times

+ 500 international stamps collected

+ Complete US mint collection

+ Walk 1,500 miles

+ 10 good mothers good sons lunches

+ 50 workouts with Derrick

+ 50x 300 abs workout

+ To 85 miles greenways

+ 60 pushups 50x

+ Scuba dive 3x

+ 100 naps

+ 20 movies

+ Chelsea home safe from Peru

+ Chelsea second year at Open Sky

+ Chelsea enroll in Smith

+ SS/MD financial plan in place

+ Sunset block fixed, house painted

+ Trust plan for grandkids' education

Juggle consciously in dream

+ Five flying dreams

+ Nikko successful school transition

+ Fitbit walk NYC to SF

+ 50 shoulder exercises

+ 12 nights of live music

+ Listen to 50 albums

+ 25x media recognition

Attend ten sporting events

+ One elite sporting event

+ Buy Sherry diamond ring/Pave
+ Buy Sherry saxophone
+ Meditate 50x
+ Dance for Safe Haven
+ *Game of Thrones* 5 seasons
+ Raise $1 million 440 Greenway

And here is a sampling from past successful lists:

Three fishing outings

Orioles to playoffs

Titans to playoffs

100 days of abstinence

15 yoga classes

Launch Village Urban Relocation

Play 5 new golf courses

Sign up 500 Go Green customers

Recruit 200 Greenways Corporate members

10 walks Radnor

Gulch Greenway implemented

10 piano lessons

Sherry MD writing vacation

25 pre-1920 US stamps

25 real estate referrals

Collect cool 1870s commemorative stamp series

To Omaha with Vandy BBall

Nikko in Encore

Whitney through Diesel College

MD play with Scattered Showers

MD .500+ batting average

Riverfront Park development started

Completely sell out 5 projects for developers

MD/Newell 53 homes sold

MD Team 400 homes sold

Get to 50 miles of greenways

Budget to pay down Sunset mortgages 1/2 time

$53m month at Village

MD to mayor's Green Team/Open Space Advisory Panel

Village $250k distributions

Defeat Maytown through 2009

SS/MD 2009 budget to Snowball income

Ecobroker designation

MD 25 agent recruiting appointments

Take surfing lessons with Mike Kempf

Excellence in Leadership

Shift the way real estate is practiced

Use RE as platform to serve country, environment

Chelsea through university year with B+ average

$51 million month

Sherry Stewart 5th future 50

LetterLogic recycled content paper and envelopes (or certified forest)

Sherry Stewart top 10 woman-owned businesses Nashville

Sherry entrepreneur of the year

Attend ULI event

Swim 51 miles

Dance, 5 lessons

Trip to Brazil, Argentina, or Chile

Attend SVN spring, or fall, or SVI

Ski 5 days, or one good adventure

Scuba diving adventure

51 gifts given

Thailand, Vietnam, or Bali, Indonesia

Chelsea enrolled in college

Join ULI

Align Village with insurance company

500 Greenways memberships

Joel Solomon alive with new kidney

Scattered Showers to city tourney 2011

#1 Biz Journal 7th straight year

Anyone can make a list like this, and with active and engaged attention, get a lot done—even in a recession. I've learned now that many innovators understand the importance of achieving goals, and research shows that high-purpose fulfillment is related to accomplishing goals frequently. In doing so, our brains are positioned to expect and celebrate successes repeatedly, leading to sustained personal fulfillment. That is what my lists have done for me, and I now have ten years of lists under my belt.

I hope that this serves as an example of the many activities and goals that can make up "the list," that it shows the value of list making, and even the value of sharing your list with your close friends. Interestingly, Dana noted that monetary goals make up just a fraction of my list. She suggested that my wealth goals should shift toward the creation of a better community-based balance sheet, with the aspiration to create mega millions in community returns. When I rally the creation of the 440 Greenway or create a trail-oriented development project, for example, I should put this on my personal balance sheet. It is an interesting concept and worthy of consideration. I'll put it on my next list!

During the time of the 2008 recession, the Werthan Mills Lofts was going through the fourth phase of the 120-unit, $28 million project. We were also under construction with the Glen, an $11 million new build project of thirty-six condo units in Hillsboro Village. And we were underway with our first cottage series, West End Station, a $12 million development. As I noted earlier, these bank debts were on my personal balance sheet. We had presold 103 units at Werthan Mills Lofts, nearly all of our homes at West End Station, and 75 percent of our condos at the Glen.

We were, with able guidance from Cory Short, the construction manager for Core at that time, in the fortunate position of being within our construction timeline and under our budget. We finished up construction in March 2008 and were able to close on seventy-eight units before the market really began to melt. We scrambled, lowering prices quickly, and sold enough units to "get out of the bank" (pay off the bank loan), leasing the rest of the units to sell another day.

We finished the Glen in the summer of 2008, and surprisingly, most of our presales closed. Indeed, I expected the rest of the sales to linger, but we were able to sell out the project in mid-2009 and did well. These sales are a resounding endorsement of the strength of walkable communities. The project is just outside of Hillsboro Village and only a couple of blocks from Vanderbilt University, in my original "one-mile radius," with its substantial endowment and a wonderful program to support student tuitions. Even in a recession, higher education thrives.

Fortunately, as I've mentioned, Core Development was moving from building condominiums into another type of product, which proved to be more recession resilient. With financial markets in turmoil, it would have been impossible to develop more condos anyway. We designed the cottage series to offer entry-level prices for homes in a fairly dense residential setting of ten to fifteen homes per acre. The detached homes have front porches that face a common green. Our first community, West End Station, was a forty-five-home community, and we had presold our first phase of twenty-four homes pre-recession. Remarkably, nearly all of these sales closed.

The cottage series generally works in an edge environment, because people there value community and detached homes, and West End Station was a perfect fit. That section of Sylvan Park had needed a boost; the five-acre parcel was located in a crook between two rail lines. The railway that separated the project from the Noah Liff Opera Center served only as a spur to manufacturing and ran just a couple of trains per day. The other line was reasonably active but in a "no-blow" zone. So, the product sold remarkably well. Given that condos were now stigmatized, these cottages were a great option. And it was a good recession-proof project, a safe haven in a turbulent real estate environment.

In 2009, Gale Park, Core Development's second cottage series, was revived. Gale Park had been conceived before West End Station but was still hampered by a drawn-out political process, and we'd been unable to get the necessary zoning change. To get through the political process, and to support the neighborhood, Core had promised to create sidewalks on a dangerous bend at Gale, thereby connecting the neighborhood to the commercial district. Linking the residential and commercial areas was vital to the success of the development. Core had also promised to support affordable housing. While the neighbors supported the plan, the councilman was not sold and seemed to favor another concept for the site, hoping to land a big box retailer. The Metropolitan Council voted in 2008 to defer Gale Park indefinitely. When a project is deferred indefinitely, it usually means it will never be approved. So when the councilman decided, for reasons unknown, to motion for approval in his last session in the Metropolitan Council, we were surprised and had to scramble to put the project back on track.

Seventy-nine-unit Gale Park, a project in Core Development's cottage series.

Gale Park emerged as a prime example of the power of the one-mile radius. It is a seven-acre site at an edge between a commercial strip, with Kroger as an anchor, and the Melrose neighborhood. As developers of Gale Park, we offloaded fifteen thousand dump trucks with the fill. As good community builders, we sent it for free to the airport, which needed fill. The $23 million project resulted in seventy-nine homes.

The project won a ULI Development in Excellence award from the Nashville chapter. The ULI cited many reasons when choosing this project for recognition: The project energized a neighborhood commercial district in the Melrose community, which continues to expand and thrive. It offered an attainable price point for two- and three-bedroom homes, with prices ranging from $239,900 to $339,900 in our original offering. The homes were energy efficient and offered residents great home performance and low energy costs. The project succeeded through a recession, and it created social development. The friendly front porches and shared greens naturally enhanced community relations. People talked to one another; they became neighbors in the real sense of the word. The project eliminated an ugly pile of more than fifteen thousand dump truck loads of dirt that was replaced by a pleasing community, easily viewed by many from the I-65/I-440 interchange. And the project was a desirable product type while nearly all of the condominium projects in Nashville were in chaos.

We fulfilled our promise of affordable housing support for the neighborhood. As the last home at Gale Park sold and closed in 2014, we reflected on the success of the project and put $475,000 into the Village Fund. The funds were earmarked for nonprofits that were involved in affordable housing initiatives, notably, HON with its Home Energy Savings (HES) program; Rebuilding Nashville Together, which helps seniors with repairs so that they can age in place; Safe Haven, which houses homeless families; and Affordable Housing Resources, which educates low-income people and families to help them buy and retain their homes.

Gale Park and a sister apartment building that Core developed across the street have led to greater considerations, such as the creation of the 440 Greenway, which would basically access the front door of the community, and the Browns Creek Greenway, which would pick up on Franklin Road, behind the Melrose post office, and give residents a chance to move about the city. These two considerations, and the development itself, show the power of the cottage series in an edge community and how it can help stimulate community within that metaphorical, but very real, one-mile radius.

Not only had our Core projects succeeded, with some good timing and fortitude, during a major recession, but Nashville's reputation as a go-to city was heating up. Good governance, our emerging collective wisdom, and, I would say, the strength and depth of emerging urban neighborhoods, allowed our city to gain traction. Around 2009, Nashville began to collect a series of endorsements that any city in the world would envy. We are all a product of our times, and I have learned that it is important to rise to the occasion. I am proud to have been deeply engaged in both Nashville's recession and resurgence.

Mayor Dean and the city took the long view and doubled down, building the Music City Center at recessionary pricing. We added downtown riverfront parks and exercised a greenways and green space plan at a time when property was most affordable. The B-Cycle bikesharing plan was formalized, along with a complete street initiative, and we pushed forward a public transportation plan (more on that later).

NASHVILLE ACCOLADES & RANKINGS

YEAR	ACCOLADE	BY	RANK
2014	Most Affordable Big Cities in the United States	Kiplinger	4
2014	Best Business Climates	*Business Facilities Magazine*	4
2014	Friendliest Cities	*Conde Nast Traveler*	8
2014	Best Places for Business and Careers	*Forbes*	10
2014	7 Great American Vacation Spots (That Won't Bust Your Budget)	*TIME*	1
2014	America's Most Creative Cities	*Forbes*	3
2014	Best Large Cities for Job Growth in 2014	NewGeography.com	6
2014	American Cities for the Young and Artistically Inclined	PolicyMic	1
2014	Best Big Cities for Jobs	*Forbes*	6
2014	America's New Brain-power Cities	Wendell Cox	4
2014	The USA's 20 Best Convention Cities	10Best.com	3
2014	Best Cities to Be an Artist	MyLife.com	6
2014	10 Most Popular Cities for Millennials	MSN Real Estate	10
2013	Cities Creating the Most Tech Jobs	*Forbes*	4
2013	Top Cities for Middle-Class Jobs	*Forbes*	7
2013	America's Top 25 Housing Investment Markets	OwnAmerica	12
2013	"Where the Jobs Are" List	CNN Money	11

2013	Best Cities for Business & Careers	*Forbes*	5
2013	Most Business-Friendly Cities	CNN Money	6
2013	Best Cities for Jobs	*Forbes*	2
2013	America's Next Boomtown City	AOL.com	1
2013	Top American Boomtowns	Bloomberg	8
2013	Best City for Young Entrepreneurs	Under30CEO.com	5
2013	10 Great Cities to Start a Business	Kiplinger	10
2013	Best Meeting Destination in the Country	Cvent Supplier Network	14
2012	America's Best Cities	Bloomberg *Businessweek*	13
2012	Best City in the Country for Business and Careers	*Forbes*	10
2012	Destination on the Rise	Trip Advisor	1
2012	Top 5 US cities with fastest-growing job market	The Atlantic Cities Place Matters	1
2011	US Comeback Cities	Kiplinger	1
2011	Best States for Making a Living	MoneyRates.com	8
2011	Best Cities for Minority Entrepreneurs	*Forbes*	3
2011	Best City for College Graduates	*Forbes*	4
2011	One of the Best Places to Retire	*Forbes*	N/A
2010	100 Best Communities for Young People	America's Promise Alliance	N/A
2010	Best Sports City	SportingNews	18
2010	Best-Performing Cities	Milken Institute	84

2010	Most Popular City in US	Harris Interactive Poll	7
2010	Most Affordable City in America	*Forbes*	5
2010	Most Friendly Environment for Entrepreneurship	SBE Council	11
2009	America's Friendliest City	*Travel + Leisure* and *Today* show	N/A
2009	No. 1 Quality of Life; No. 6 Best Cost of Living; No. 9 Economic Growth Potential	Business Facilities	N/A

The recession reset the condominium market and set the stage for eight years of multifamily apartment development. Progressive companies took notice and shifted resources to our city. Our Entrepreneur Center was churning out lots of smart, young tech companies, and millennials decided to move in. In the aftermath and reset, housing in the city and in surrounding neighborhoods became highly desirable, and new build in-fill became the norm. Nashville learned to discover emerging neighborhoods faster. The economy and outlook for condos brightened. Icon in the Gulch, which we originally sold at $353 per square foot, dropped to $310 per square foot in the recession but now tops $475 per square

Richland Station, a 40 unit Core cottage series project in Sylvan Park

foot. Those buyers who closed and held on have been rewarded for their fortitude.

New problems also emerged for developers—for example, the permitting process slowed under the strain, becoming one of the biggest hurdles for a new project. As one might expect, the public sector involved in permitting, planning, and codes is overworked, and there is a growing backlog of projects needing their consideration. Making it worse, as the real estate development market heated, or even overheated, the private sector hired away many of the best planners and zoning specialists from the public sector. At Core Development's most recent annual strategic planning session, we identified the slowing permitting process as our number-one business threat for the year.

Conversation about how to get the city to pay more for codes, planning, and permitting officials, or to outsource these functions to the private sector, abound. There is even talk about a fast-tracking process, where a developer would have the ability to pay a "significant impact fee" to streamline inspections. This was something that was originally proposed by the Green Ribbon Commission under Karl Dean, with proceeds to go to environmental stewardship. We were in a recession then, and it never happened, but it should be considered once again in 2017, perhaps with proceeds going to the Barnes Fund for Affordable Housing. With over $3 billion of building projects in the pipeline, the city needs to realize the huge opportunity cost we'll incur in lost time, for investors and customers, not to mention the delayed impact on our communities. The property taxes on these projects alone could also be a tremendous boon to the city's coffers.

This does bring up a question that many developers may not want to address, which is "when is so much growth not a good thing?" For the most part, I believe that community-oriented development is almost always a good thing, especially when reclaiming the urban spaces that were lost in prior generations, or when repurposing underutilized urban industrial spaces to add services and vitality. There are instances, though, where it makes intuitive sense to slow down. When Studio B, a building on Music Row with a rich history of legendary recordings, was in danger of being demolished for another apartment building, our community reacted. Shouldn't we be preserving our music heritage, given our strong creative culture, tourist industry, and Music City moniker? What is the future of Music Row? When the "tall skinny" in-fill development in East Nashville ran amok, the community also reacted. Shouldn't we be preserving the stock of affordable housing and make it more difficult to demolish the current housing stock? Is this trend accelerating gentrification? Even in emerging neighborhoods where the creative class has studios and workshops, new development brings its challenges. Does the new development of housing, restaurants, and even pricier galleries encroach on the affordability for these artists and makers?

The recession coupled with the great flood of 2010 was a thought-provoking time for our city and for me personally. Our collective response set the stage for the flurry of activity that was to come. It took its toll, but hardships can have silver linings in that they build community, too. People helped people and learned to live with less. Churches, civic groups, and the citizens in Nashville and Tennessee, the Volunteer State, worked to survive and to help those who were less fortunate. In many households, adult children came home and stayed for a time, as jobs were scarce, and families stuck together. Our community of Village agents, now tightly engaged in our home office on Twenty-First Avenue South, did what we could for each other, and for our community, and weathered the storm. Needless to say, now that condominiums were stigmatized and stymied, the

Village multi-residential sales plan I wrote of previously, and thereby our company's growth into other cities, fell by the wayside. Perhaps in this we were even lucky.

Chapter 8

Going Green

Dense, compact cities are the way forward in the development of man, and are critical to combating climate change and inequality.

—Lord Richard Rogers,
Urban Land Institute

IN THE MID-1990S, I got a call from my friend and teacher Reta, who was taking a group of Buddhists on a tour of the high Andes in Peru. Her translator had become ill, and she asked if I would please come to Peru (in two weeks!) to translate. Though I have a college degree in Spanish, I was nervous that it was not up to the level of what was needed for this gig. And two weeks! I had a busy career. But really, how could I refuse? This was to be a sixteen-day journey, traveling through Lima to Cuzco and then to parts beyond. We would be traveling with Don Américo Yábar, one of the famous guardians of the sacred mountains, and with his son, a budding shaman, Gayle Yábar. We would be visiting sacred sites, many of them ruins of the ancient Inca.

Don Américo with Gayle and Reta.

Don Américo in front of the mysterious Peruvian landmark "Puerta de Hayu Marka" (Doorway of the Amaru Meru). Photo courtesy of Kenneth Robinson.

We met Don Américo shortly after arriving. We had hiked and climbed up over the city of Cuzco and stopped at a rock outcropping. He appeared, taking in the group and his new translator. He circled us up, put me on his right and Reta on his left, and began a discourse, which I translated. Don Américo was gentle, spoke slowly with good breaks for translation, and let me catch up with him as he spoke. I could feel that he was going to take good care of me and the group.

While I was focused on the linguistics, Don Américo focused on the energy. He worked with me to ensure that my translation reflected his energy. If he was speaking quietly, he wanted my translation delivered in a whisper. If he was projecting his presence, I had to make my translation big and powerful. It was a beautiful feeling of merging with another human being, of letting go of myself and really combining forces with someone else, an example of deep camaraderie.

Our days consisted of traveling with our fine bus driver, Dante, to one of the sacred sites. We would hike into the site, often a place with astounding rock formations and Incan ruins, and find a place to do the work. The work involved meditation, connecting to the Pachamama, or mother earth, absorbing the teachings of Don Américo, and plenty of reflection. We often had interactions with the Peruvian people. The Incan culture was prevalent throughout the northern Andes for eight hundred years but began to dissipate and be assimilated into the emerging European culture in the 1500s. The people in the high Andes, though, still have the unique look of the indigenous culture. They are gentle, and live simply and close to the earth.

At one point, we journeyed to see the Q'ero, a clan that lives in the mountains at an elevation of approximately fifteen thousand feet. They had walked down to meet us, which was more than a day's journey, and we met at about fourteen thousand feet. The weather was surreal, and the skies and the clouds were like a dream. The interaction was astounding. This clan spoke only Quechua, with Don Américo translating to Spanish, me to English, and back again.

The Q'ero and their leader, El Presidente, spoke of global warming and of how, at fifteen thousand feet, they felt the effects of worldwide climate change. The snowmelt meant that their cold season was shorter. When the snow melted early, their llamas' gums bled. This had a great impact on their lifestyle. They told us they had radios where they lived, and they could tune in to events happening around the planet. They knew that everything is connected.

Don Américo, as he often did in our interactions with the people of Peru, asked me to juggle for El Presidente. I stood up, threw my balls in the air, and missed them all. I was astounded and tried again, with the same result. Why was I not able to juggle? I felt that I was in a dreamlike state. I tried yet again, and the balls flew out, landing on the lap of El Presidente. I asked him to keep them as a gift, and he simply asked what was inside them.

"Seeds," I said. "Perhaps I'll plant them," said El Presidente. I'll never know why I wasn't able to juggle, though I know from experience that I'm unable to catch the balls when I try to juggle in my dreams. Hmmm. That trip wound up being one of the most remarkable of my life. It solidified the idea that everything we do on this side of the world affects the other side.

Climate change is not some concocted dream or fabricated story. Recall in Nashville the Great Flood of 2010, when Mother Nature dumped seventeen inches of rain on the city, the highest amount in more than 140 years of recorded history. Thirteen of those inches poured down in the first thirty-six hours, more than doubling the previous two-day rainfall record set in 1979. There was so much water that the Cumberland River crested in Nashville at 51.86 feet, twelve feet above flood stage.

I was showing homes on that Saturday, a couple of days before the Cumberland crested, and had lined up twelve homes for some relocating out-of-towners. The rain was just pouring down, all day, but my buyers were troopers. In perhaps a preview of what was to come, we arrived at one of the homes, near Browns Creek off of Woodmont, and found a sign at the door, "No showings, house flooding." Browns Creek was already over its banks, and the level of groundwater pouring into basements without sump pumps was astonishing.

Aftermath of the Great Flood of 2010.

Over the next couple of days, I continued to survey the scene, driving around to watch the waters rise. I went down to the Titans' Stadium and watched the Cumberland as it rose up and spilled its banks, and then went back across the river as Lower Broadway began to flood. I could have kayaked through the streets.

The damage was horrific. According to the Metro Planning Department, and the Codes Administration, the flood resulted in an estimated $2 billion in damages to private property. Ten thousand people were displaced from their homes and nearly eleven thousand properties were damaged or destroyed in the flooding.

But just as happened after the tornado, the flood offered a chance to see Nashville's incredible community rise to the challenge. Hands On Nashville, under Brian Williams' stewardship, became a primary organizing force, coordinating more than twenty-five thousand volunteers in flood relief efforts and organizing to help affected households with the many issues that flooding creates, from emptying homes of damaged goods, to stream and community cleanup.

It was a remarkable time. Huge piles of debris lined the streets, bigger piles in the most impacted zones. Even in neighborhoods without a nearby creek or river, houses were damaged when the groundwater spilled into finished spaces below grade. Some neighborhoods, like Bellevue, were severely impacted, perhaps because much of that neighborhood was built in the five-hundred-year floodplain. When shopping for homes for the next several years, and even today, the question became "Did the house flood in 2010?"

When the water subsided, new policies were instituted that had an impact on floodplains. Flooded properties in lowlands were bought out, demolished, and turned into new greenways and parks. So, in fact, Mother Nature wound up helping the green-up project. Nashville, now sensitive to the devastating impact of rising waters, is better situated as we continue to deter development in the floodplains and develop parkland downtown with flood walls, and as we shift from asphalt to greenways and parks in some of our fast-growing neighborhoods.

Much like the orcas, those killer whales that I studied in my younger days, we may attempt to adapt to the climate changes. The orcas simply push north as the ice opens up with the arctic melt. They hunt narwhals, bowheads, and beluga. Some of the native people appreciate the killer whale, as orca hunting tactics push the narwhal to shore, making it easy for the Inuit to hunt. But, as I witnessed in the Johnstone Strait, orcas often hunt beyond need and will decimate a population even if not hungry, so relations with the Inuit may change over time as the whales deplete the narwhal population, and the Inuit too may be victims of the climate shift.

One of the discussions that the Urban Land Institute is having with leaders throughout the organization has to do with climate resiliency. Many cities are having weather events, from tidal surges on the coasts to drought in the West, newly forming tornado alleys in the Midwest and South to extreme heat in the Midwest. Cities, planners, and developers are grappling with these issues in different ways, depending on what is most likely to have an impact in their unique conditions. Chicago residents, for instance, have realized that they are subject to a rising number of deadly one-hundred-degree days and have been greening asphalt jungles and roofs across the city in an attempt to lessen the impact on their citizens. Coastal cities, such as New York City, are looking at ways to channel tidal surge and considering ways to create permeable edge zones.

Orcas in the Johnston Straight assessing the surroundings. This behavior is known as "spy hopping".

In Nashville, we are fortunate to have been chosen in 2016 to be one of the 100 Resilient Cities (100RC), with a grant from the Rockefeller Foundation. The grant will help our city become more resilient—defined as the capacity of individuals, communities, institutions, businesses, and systems in a city to survive, adapt, and grow no matter what the chronic stresses and acute shocks they experience. A panel of expert judges reviewed over a thousand applications from prospective cities around the world. The judges looked for innovative mayors, recent examples of change due to catalyzing events, a history of building partnerships, and an ability to work with a wide range of stakeholders. The process in Nashville resulted in the naming of Erik Cole as chief resilience officer in the Mayor's Office. It's an amazing opportunity to bring focus to Nashville's efforts to develop a city that can handle whatever climate change—or Mother Earth—throws at us.

Gregor Roberson, mayor of Vancouver.

Learning how other cities are dealing with climate resiliency will influence how we learn and respond. My friend Gregor Robertson ran for mayor of Vancouver on a platform that declared the city should be "the greenest city in the world." In 2008, when he won, Gregor recruited Sadhu Johnston, a rock star in the world of sustainability. Sadhu had laid down some immense changes in Chicago during the years he served as director of sustainability under Mayor Richard M. Daley and had developed strategies for greening roofs, alternative transportation, and resiliency. As the new city manager of

Vancouver, with a position that was senior to public works and planning, Sadhu ensured that sustainability was imbedded in all aspects of governance. (Note that Vancouver has also been selected in 2016 as one of the 100RC.) Reminding us of the pattern that connects, I originally met Gregor on Cortes Island, where he lived with his family and when he was involved with Hollyhock. And Sadhu happens to be the son of Pria, who is married to Thomas. Thomas and Reta were our Alaya trainers in Nashville in the early 1990s, and it was Reta who took me to the high Andes. There is always a pattern that connects, especially in Nashville.

One of the first things Sadhu did post-election was to map Vancouver's energy usage and to target the heaviest users. The Molson Brewery, at the edge of downtown, was at the top of the list. Beyond heavy energy usage, the factory also generated a lot of waste, especially discarded hops, which had to be trucked away. City representatives went to Molson, studied its output, and came up with a better strategy. They showed Molson how a newly created powerhouse, fed by the discarded hops, could be used to run the entire factory. And this powerhouse would have overflow energy for consumption in the surrounding neighborhood! It was a win/win/win, and it saved Molson lots of money. I loved the idea and wondered what tangible steps we could take in Nashville to similarly reduce our energy consumption.

Ed McMahon, a senior fellow at ULI, spoke to the Nashville chapter in 2008. He noted that approximately 45 percent of Nashville's energy was consumed by buildings, while New York, a very compact city, was at 70 percent. More than 40 percent of America's carbon emissions in fact come from heating, cooling, lighting, and operating buildings. In neighborhoods characterized by unique and historic homes, such as many found throughout Nashville, that percentage is even higher.

McMahon also noted that 85 percent of the buildings existing today will still exist in 2030. You can imagine how I leaned forward at that statement! He spoke about the incredible energy savings that can be had when retrofitting older structures, as most were built without much concern for energy efficiency. In fact, most older buildings are energy sieves. Energy efficiency had not been a concern back then, and even homes and neighborhoods built in the 1980s and 1990s are not efficient. By retrofitting these homes to increase their energy efficiency, the homes become less dependent on fossil fuels, and the community's carbon footprint shrinks.

After hearing McMahon's speech, I talked with ULI leadership and volunteered to chair a sustainability committee. We invited the group responsible for retrofitting the Empire State Building in New York City to talk to our ULI chapter. With a $500 million capital improvement program underway, the building's ownership was working with the Clinton Global Change initiative and had decided to use the iconic Empire State Building as a case study to prove or disprove the economic viability of whole-building energy efficiency retrofits. The information they shared with us was motivating and astounding. At its current energy costs, the retrofit of the Empire State Building had reduced energy usage by 38 percent, creating savings of a minimum of 105,000 metric tons of CO_2 over the next fifteen years. The building sector must be an integral part of the climate change solution, given that it is the largest contributor to US greenhouse gas emissions.

In Nashville, we decided first to focus on homes, recognizing an immediate opportunity to attain tangible results while educating our community about the power of sustainability. Our group picked the Hillsboro Village neighborhood, known in the Metropolitan Council as District 18, to begin our work. My sense was that this was a neighborhood where people were already aware, and I lived there as well, making it easy for me to be engaged. Our stated goal was to support Mayor Dean's initiative in the report of the 2009 Green Ribbon Committee on Environmental Sustainability. That report had set goals of a 5 percent reduction in energy use by 2012 and a 20 percent reduction in energy use by 2020. Back to work within a one-mile radius of Hillsboro Village!

The Tennessee Valley Authority (TVA), which creates energy for our region, and the Nashville Electric Service (NES), our local electric service provider, had an incentive program offering homeowners an energy evaluation of their residence. If a homeowner did $1,000 worth of the recommended work, the TVA would give them $500. NES worked with us, analyzing the neighborhood. We set a goal of 360 energy retrofits and kicked off a campaign.

Sherry and I signed up to have our home audited. We were embarrassed when our auditor pointed out all of the gaps, realizing that our home, which was over a hundred years old, was an energy sieve. He talked about the chimney effect, and the importance of keeping the energy from rising up from our basement and out of our roof, and estimated that we'd save 8 percent of our energy outlay by insulating our basement, another 7 percent if we sealed our existing ductwork, and another 7 percent if we insulated our attic. We got our work done and felt good, as good stewards do, that we were reducing our carbon footprint. We were equally pleased to receive a $500 TVA rebate and to see a calculation that these savings were going to pay back our energy-reducing expenditure in less than five years.

This was something that we could sell! We got Kristine LaLonde, who was running for office in District 18, behind the cause, and coined our rallying cry, "Go Green District 18." We officially kicked off the campaign with Mayor Dean and neighborhood leaders, and Mayor Dean expressed his desire that Nashville be the "greenest city in the Southeast."

The ULI Sustainability Committee recruited many volunteers, and we went door to door, held seminars, and set up tables and booths in visible locations, giving people an opportunity to sign up. NES and the TVA got behind the cause, providing yard signage and marketing material. "Go Green" signs started to pop up throughout the neighborhood.

This was a perfect opportunity for Village agents to engage in the community. Helping people improve energy efficiency was nonthreatening and service oriented. Our office in the middle of District 18 served as the command center where meetings and volunteer groups assembled.

When I was canvassing, I could sign up about four people per hour for an energy evaluation, whether knocking on doors or standing at a table in front of the local grocery store. Half of those folks actually went through with the whole process without further prompting. Some needed follow-up, which was another good excuse to make a call. Like so many things, what is good for the neighborhood—and the earth—is often good for business!

I called back one family who had signed up for the audit on Clayton Avenue and found they'd had a successful audit and were thrilled with the results. Encouraged by such enthusiasm, I asked them for a testimonial. They were happy to provide one and added that the wife was pregnant with twins, so they needed a bigger place but wanted to stay in the neighborhood. Might I be able to help them? Of course, I could, and I put on my real estate hat, sold their home, and found them another. The home we sold was valued at $575,000, and the home they bought, a home that Newell Anderson and I were listing, was valued at $800,000. What a wonderful bonus for doing community work!

Kristine LaLonde was elected as our new District 18 councilwoman and told the story of our success in a Metropolitan Council meeting and issued a challenge. Several council people rose to the occasion. Councilman Mike Jameson accepted on behalf of his East Nashville constituency, with the catchy slogan, "District 6 Energy Fix." Jason Holleman accepted for Sylvan Park, with "Green to the Core District 24." Sean McGuire accepted for Green Hills, with "Greener Hills." And Erik Cole accepted for Inglewood with "Energy Heaven in District 7." Our committee was pleased with the spirit of competition and loved the creativity. We expanded our campaign and created more signs and marketing materials (see following pages for examples).

Over time, four additional council districts participated in the launch of Go Green North Nashville. In partnership with Tennessee State University, Go Green secured an $800,000 grant from HUD to retrofit North Nashville homes. This initiative was led by Ginger Hausser, a Hillsboro Village neighbor who had served as our District 18 Metropolitan Nashville councilwoman for eight years and was working as the assistant director and HUD grant manager for

district 6
energy fix

ENERGY
HEAVEN
DISTRICT 7

SAVING green
IN DISTRICT 17

GREEN TO THE CORE
DISTRICT 24

go Green
TIME
district 29

dreaming
GREEN
IN DISTRICT 19

DISTRICTS 25 & 34
Greener
Hills

N
GO GREEN
north nashville

District 18 Door Hanger

TVA / District 18 Advertisement

District 18 Yard Sign

Go Green Nashville Website

District 18
NES Electric Bill Insert

Tennessee State University. She leveraged her influence to impact the neighborhoods near the campus with the Go Green campaign. This grant was used to deeply retrofit and repair one hundred low-income households that would otherwise be unable to afford the cost. Hands On Nashville (HON) was chosen to implement the energy retrofit work, and it was for this work that it created its internal program, Home Energy Savings (HES).

The HUD grant helped aging homeowners stay in their homes. One of the biggest costs that aging homeowners incur is their energy bill. Often, these homeowners have paid off their mortgage but face the prospect of having to leave their home because of the cost of energy and maintenance. This program allowed many poor seniors to age in place, which has so many tangible benefits, including maintaining social and community ties.

One day when our Sustainability Committee was talking about energy issues in the back room at Fido, the Bongo World coffeehouse in Hillsboro Village, I was introduced to Professor James Fraser. I learned that he and his Vanderbilt graduate students had been doing a study of households in the Chestnut Hill neighborhood in District 17, which he described as the lowest-earning district in Davidson County. Many of these homes, he said, had no mortgages, but because of very low household income, these neighbors were struggling. The homes were in generally poor condition, and utility assistance was the number one need.

Bingo. As we finished our coffee, I told James about the work we'd been doing, and we pulled together a plan, working with HON/HES to retrofit fifty homes. The Village Fund leveraged monies, got additional grants from the ULI and a Cities of Service grant, and raised $128,000. This money paid for materials, and HON managed the volunteer teams. We used the information for the Vanderbilt studies to identify homes, and HON vetted them for the program.

When HON schedules retrofits using this program, the nonprofit asks that a support group bring eight good workers out for each home. It continues to schedule two to three homes on a Saturday, and the work runs about four hours. Supervisors at each home train the workforce, and everyone gets their hands a little dirty. The day starts with a blower door test, which measures the airflow turnover in the home. The premise is that if the airflow is reduced, the home will then be more efficient.

In each home, the volunteers perform a full scope of work. This includes attic insulation; weather stripping for doors and windows; low-flow shower heads and sink aerators; compact fluorescent lighting; insulated blankets for water heaters; insulation for hot water pipes; tape and mastic on heating, ventilation, and air-conditioning (HVAC) ducts; carbon monoxide and smoke detectors; and reusable air filters. Project managers oversee the process and do some of the work that requires professional expertise, such as HVAC tune-ups.

The HON/HES program now has a proven track record of success, reducing homeowners' utility bills by an average of 16 percent. This makes a real difference in the lives of low-income homeowners and makes the home safer and more comfortable. As a volunteer, the work is very satisfying, and Village loves to support and put together work teams.

This program got a nice financial boost when in 2012 Greg Gillum—a Village customer and good neighbor—started a closed-course road race he called the 12South Winter WarmUp. 12South is the now-affluent neighborhood located in the same district as Chestnut Hill. Greg came to Village and asked me to sponsor the effort, letting me know that all proceeds from the event would benefit a neighborhood cause. Together with Greg's team, we decided that the recipient of the funds would be HON/HES, with funding used to help with our retrofit project in Chestnut Hill. The event was a success, with over three hundred runners participating, and was a strong financial boost for the retrofit initiative in District 17. It has continued to build momentum, and in 2016 the event hosted over 1,000 runners, including 175 young runners in a kid's run! The event has solidified a neighborhood alliance with HON, which will now be the permanent recipient of the funding.

With tracking help from the Nashville Energy Works in the mayor's sustainability office, Go Green shared its results. I was pleased to see that 3,850 homeowners had signed up for the energy evaluation and 1,900 retrofits had been performed. Individual homeowners had spent on average about $5,400 on their energy retrofit, generating a total of $6.6 million in homeowner investment. Go Green Home Services is now officially housed as a subsidiary of Village, and we work with our agents to help them educate their clients on how to create a healthier, more sustainable, and more affordable home through energy upgrades.

We can still do more. Village is furthering its relationship with HON to help identify and address some of our community's unmet needs within the school district. We have developed a three-pronged approach that includes engaging low-income residents, volunteers, schools, and local nonprofits. The year 2015 marked the third year working with HON in District 17. The current initiative completed another fifty-two energy-efficiency upgrade projects in homes. Additionally, we tackled energy-reducing initiatives in schools and nonprofits. Four area schools—Fall-Hamilton Enhanced Option Elementary, Carter Lawrence Elementary, Cameron College Preparatory, and Johnson Alternative Learning Center—were selected. The goal was to create a safer learning environment with better lighting and air quality and to use the program to create a dynamic learning experience through sustainability.

A number of area nonprofits were also selected to receive smart building technologies and energy upgrades: Harvest Hands Community Development Corporation, FiftyForward, Casa Azafrán, South Nashville Action People, W.O. Smith Music School, Rochelle Center, Operation Stand Down Tennessee, and Safe Haven Family Shelter. Audits and energy upgrades were completed using Go Green Home Services. Using diagnosis from the audits, these nonprofits received a prioritized scope of work. The hope is that the nonprofits will take the energy savings from this work to put toward further recommendations. This is something that Metropolitan Nashville Public School parents and nonprofit supporters can rally around. It's all about home, neighborhood, and community. Village, Core, and the Village Fund are exploring other neighborhoods for our continued work and partnership with HON/HES.

Want to do your part to support clean renewable energy? Make the Green Power Switch, which allows you to purchase renewable energy generated in the Tennessee Valley for as little as $4 more on your monthly bill. Sign up at www.tva.com/Energy/Renewable-Energy-Solutions/Green-Power-Switch.

Additionally, Hands On Nashville is always looking for volunteers for the HES program, and you will be happy to lend your time and energy. Visit www.hon.org for more information.

In 2014, the Tennessee Environmental Council (TEC) honored me with the Sustainable Tennessee award for my work with these various greening initiatives. Bob Freeman, who is on the board, notified me of the award, and when presenting it said, "There are reasons that Nashville has become one of the most desirable, vibrant places to live in all of America. And tonight's award winner is one of those reasons. Mark weaves the concepts of sustainability into the fabric of his thriving business. Mark has been active with the TEC in the past. We remember him when he used to auction his service for the sale of a home, with all proceeds benefitting the TEC. He did that for many years, generally juggling while the auctioneer sold the service!" I love that juggling continues to serves as an apt metaphor in my life.

Mayor Barry has renewed our city's commitment to be the greenest city in the Southeast. Her stated goal: create a new sustainability strategy to protect and enhance Nashville's natural resources. Barry's Livable Nashville Committee, to which I was appointed, was assigned by the mayor to "build on the successes" of Mayor Dean's 2008 Green Ribbon Committee as well as the sustainability policy work achieved in 2015 through NashvilleNext. Committee members were assigned to five subcommittees, including Natural Resources, Mobility, Waste Reduction and Recycling, Green Buildings, and Climate and Energy. I worked with the Mobility group, because of my work for greenways, and with the Climate and Energy committee. Recommendations from these subcommittees were released in early 2017, and our city has joined the table of champions, twenty-one cities across the world that have pledged to reduce our energy usage by 80 percent by 2050.

The timing couldn't be better; we have to do our best to act at the municipal level. Mayor Barry is also a signatory to the Compact of Mayors, the world's largest cooperative effort among mayors and city officials to reduce greenhouse gas emissions, track progress, and prepare for the impacts of climate change. Many cities are now pledging to be net-zero and showing their commitment to use only renewable energy. In 2016, when Saint Petersburg, Florida, pledged to become net zero by 2035, Sierra Club executive director Michael Brune issued the following statement: "The movement for clean energy in cities and towns across the country is now more important than ever. Saint Petersburg joins nineteen other cities from San Diego, California to Greensburg, Kansas that will lead the way to support equitable and inclusive communities built on 100 percent clean, renewable energy for all. Whether you're from a red state or blue state, clean energy works for everyone and local leaders will continue to move forward to create more jobs, stronger communities, and cleaner air and water." It's ironic that Saint Petersburg allocated $250,000 of the BP Oil settlement funds that they received to support their "Integrated Sustainability Action Plan."

If Nashville wants to continue to strive to be the greenest city in the Southeast, and to fulfill the recent Livable Nashville pledge, we need to continue to tackle building energy retrofits on office, industrial, institutional, and residential structures—still the low-hanging fruit—and we need to enhance our focus on using renewables to power our buildings. I am also hoping the solar movement gets more traction and support. In 2016, the NDP (Nashville Downtown Partnership) invited Tony Seba to keynote their annual meeting. Tony, the author of *Clean Disruption of Energy and Transportation*, suggests that manufacturing costs of photovoltaics (PV) and batteries are decreasing so dramatically that fossil fuels will no longer be competitive by 2030. Solar, of course, is a renewable resource, with little waste or secondary environmental cost. Fossil fuels, from coal to natural gas, require continuous extraction, which is costly, and create many additional and wasteful environmental costs. Tony made the point that, once you can install a solar array and use it for your energy at a cost lower than other sources, why would you do otherwise?

The good news is that the sun will continue to shine, and the marginal cost of the energy is zero. With more efficient batteries, it's already possible to store solar energy for use during "peak energy" periods, when the cost of energy from our utility companies is most expensive. That alone will become disruptive, as utility companies begin to lose the battle for market share. If the true cost and global impact of carbon output were factored into the equation, fossil fuels would soon fade, simply due to economics. As many in the clean energy world are advocating, we would then "leave it in the ground." Village is now looking at Go Green 2.0, and we hope that the decreasing cost of solar technology, such as the new solar shingles that are being developed by Elon Musk, the founder of Tesla and Solar City, will make it cost effective to put the sun to work in our quest to positively impact carbon output and sustainability in our city.

Tony also notes that other "smart" devices—from our smartphones to products like the Google "Nest" thermostat—have immediate energy-use impact. Installing a $299 Nest thermostat, for instance, monitors household energy use and can immediately help save up to 50 percent of home heating bills. More are coming, and they have cumulative impact in lowering future costs for all. Today's thermostats can collect data and utilize customer insights to build the energy management platform for tomorrow.

Entire countries are making the switch to renewables to power the building stock. Germany, a country with half the sunshine of the United States, has been leading the way, and solar now accounts for 20–35 percent of energy usage on a sunny day. Australia is closing the gap, and now 2.6 million Australians, or 11 percent of the population, have rooftop solar systems. Japan and China have closed the gap and have also become leaders in adding solar capacity. The United States has lagged but is now not far behind. In Denmark, the world's largest wind market, 11 percent of energy is now derived from wind. Wind, like solar, is renewable; the marginal cost of the energy is zero, and wind technology costs continue to drop dramatically.

The ability to finance these technologies will have a profound long-term impact, particularly for the residential transformation. Taking a cue from the car industry, we need to remember that the proliferation of cars in the United States did not really happen until customers could buy a car with a low down payment and pay over time. Seba calls this the $1 trillion finance opportunity, and notes that there are now solar real estate investment trusts (REITs), participatory financing methods, and city-backed bond programs emerging that will allow customers to install a solar array and pay for it over time with the energy savings it generates. Companies like SunEdison offer programs to finance, install, own, and maintain the solar array on a home.

One program that was an excellent initiative but disliked by the gas and oil lobbyists was the Property Assessed Clean Energy (PACE). This program leverages energy cost reductions to finance energy efficiency upgrades and renewable energy installations, tying it to residential property taxes. Because the savings from a PV installation continue beyond just one homeowner, to the thirty-year lifetime of these installations, these programs are tied to the property tax assessment and allow the current homeowner and all the future owners to enjoy the savings.

PACE originated in California, spreading to twenty-three states before it came to a halt. The Federal Housing Financing Agency, which oversees Fannie Mae and Freddie Mac, suggested that PACE loans pose "unusual lending challenges" for these lending bodies, even though statistics suggested that there was only a 1.1 percent default rate on these loans to date. That is to say, the oil and gas lobbies still have their strong voice in Washington. PACE is beginning a comeback, though, and Missouri has just okayed it, with Georgia and Arkansas close behind. Residential solar and energy retrofits would scale quickly in our country if PACE got the national nod.

In the commercial world, big box businesses, like IKEA and Walmart, are ahead of the curve. Both businesses are putting solar on 100 percent of their stores throughout the United States, which will more than power their stores. Is it possible that we might someday buy our energy from Walmart? Warren Buffett, who is often ahead of the curve, used a company that he owns to purchase a solar power plant. What does Buffett know? He says that he likes to buy boring businesses that generate cash for decades.

The reason I think about this stuff is because I'd like to make an impact, in a big way, on the cumulative carbon footprint of humans on this planet. My hope is that Nashville learns from all these initiatives, jumps in ahead of the curve, and uses the tools at our disposal to support and enhance Go Green initiatives and to go "net-zero." In pursuit of this, I have been involved with the Greater Nashville Realtors (GNR) for many years. This trade association provides Realtors, the trade name for real estate agents, with educational and professional development opportunities, dispute resolution for members and those whom they serve, legislative involvement, and communication with members for networking and growth.

The GNR has been an important part of my career. Early on, I engaged with them as a budding salesman and enjoyed participating in the GNR Awards of Excellence, always challenging myself to compete at the top of the charts. Later, I committed to various committees and learned about the workings of the organization. I was appointed chair of the newly formed Environmental Committee, where I convinced leadership that sustainability, green housing, and smart growth, topics of increasing importance to our home buyers and sellers, were therefore now also important issues for our membership.

The GNR tracks home sales in Middle Tennessee each month, with data provided by RealTracs Solutions, our local multiple listing system (MLS). The consumer can use this system to search for homes, and the Realtors have an enhanced version at their disposal. This system, at the time, lacked data about green and energy features in a home. The first thing we tackled on the Environmental Committee was the greening of the MLS. Anna Altic, a Village agent, led the task force.

When RealTracs adopted our recommendations, it immediately became one of the greenest MLS systems in the nation. It added a host of home feature options that can be selected when an agent or customer lists them in their search criteria. These include home ratings such as Energy Star and LEED, and home features such as low-E windows, the R-value of insulation, and the SEER rating of an HVAC system. The consumer option to select these energy features during their search is beginning to have an impact on the building trade, and their influence will continue to grow as builders learn more about consumers' energy-saving habits.

At the GNR Awards of Excellence event in March 2014, Richard Courtney took the podium and presented me with the Community Service Award. This award is given to Realtors who have influenced our greater Nashville community and Realtor community in an important and meaningful way. Richard noted my influence as a community builder in Nashville and as a champion for sustainability through my work at Greenways for Nashville and with Go

Green. I had just stepped down from the executive committee and the board, and I appreciated the recognition in front of my peers. Brian Copeland, who is the chief engagement officer at Village, is serving as the president of the Tennessee Association of Realtors in 2016–2017, and is looking to use this local platform to build on these sustainability initiatives at the state level.

My obsession with green initiatives has even entered the personal arena. When we started dating, Sherry called me a tree hugger. I was asking about LetterLogic and sustainability, such as waste, and where paper was sourced. She wasn't happy with this line of conversation, and noted that her business was a start-up, and that for now she was most concerned about her bottom line. She didn't have the resources to think about environmental things. But, as with many great entrepreneurs, she thought about it and began to research the possibilities and alternatives.

LetterLogic prints over five million envelopes and statements every month. Her industry as a whole has not been very progressive, and these printings have typically been on paper made from old-growth forest. The machinery that she uses, which is common across the industry, has never been adapted to work with a fully recycled paper product. So one of the first things that Sherry did was figure out how she could use sustainably developed forest products, and she made the switch.

LetterLogic was filling a couple of big dumpsters with trash per month, and her employees had begun to notice and care. One suggested how they could recycle some of this waste, and Sherry acknowledged him with a monetary award for his idea. They now not only recycle the waste but actually have people who pick it up and pay for what was once trash. LetterLogic gives the money it receives for these spoils back to the local community. The employees get to pick the nonprofit recipients, and they favor the ones in the neighborhood, like Safe Haven. Although the company is now much larger, it still only fills half of a dumpster with trash per month because of all of the recycling it achieves.

LetterLogic employees get ready to give 'mama bear', a letter truck, to Safe Haven.

Unfortunately, even with initiatives like these, climate change issues abound, hurting those who are the most vulnerable. Ten of the hottest years on record have happened in the past fifteen years. We must change, for our children and the planet. We are the first generation to feel the impact of climate change and the last to do anything about it. The impact of rising seas will likely impact low-lying coastal areas across the globe and may cause disruptive, and complex, social migration. There are many things that we can do as a nation, given that we are one of the top polluters on the planet, to slow the impact, to reduce our carbon output; but this will take political will.

It might be more useful to take a cue from ULI and to speak of climate resiliency, a more neutral term, to acknowledge that the globe is heating up, in order to elicit a proper response from our leaders. President Obama did his part late in his presidency, by signing on the international climate change accord, and by using what he had at his disposal, the executive decree, to reduce carbon emissions through the Environmental Protection Agency, but that initiative may be gutted. And Bernie Sanders, in the 2016 election cycle, elevated the conversation with a new wave of supporters, saying that climate change is the number one issue that we face today. But neither is now in charge.

While I am hopeful that our national and global political leadership continue to recognize the need for vigilance, and that our nation aligns with other nations to reduce the impact that human consumption of fossil fuels is having on the planet, I remain focused on the one-mile radius, my city, my state, and my region. I hope that Tennessee and certainly Nashville continues to support alternative sources of energy and to show national leadership. On election night, November 8th, 2016, I was at a gathering of leaders and neighbors at Mayor Barry's home. A group of us watched into the evening as Donald Trump moved toward victory, consolidating the House and Senate in the process. As I left the gathering, I said to the mayor, "It's all about the city"—keeping our eye on what we can do in terms of local initiatives is one of the best ways we can feel a sense of control and empowerment in changing times.

Chapter 9

Stewards of the City

Researchers have discovered
a new wonder drug for your
health...it's called walking.

—Dr. Bob Sallis,
Kaiser Permanente

BEFORE I MOVED to Nashville, I had never really lived in a city. Yet, most of my work today revolves around cities, shaping healthy communities in that proverbial "one-mile radius." I have focused my work in our city but draw inspiration from others. Sherry and I love to travel and particularly enjoy exploring other cities. We have traveled together now to dozens of American cities and have been intentionally traveling to the old European and South American cities. Neither Sherry nor I love the materialism of the Christmas experience in the states (made for each other, MFEO!) and usually depart on December 23rd for our winter wander, returning on the 5th or so of January. We like to go somewhere, settle in, and really explore a city. We've been to Athens, Rome, Barcelona, Berlin, Lisbon, Dublin, Paris, Amsterdam, Istanbul, Prague, Buenos Aires, and Rio de Janeiro on these holiday getaways. Many of these cities, like Nashville, have a central water feature, a river or an ocean, or another prominent feature, like a mountain range, which creates a sense of place.

We have noted that many of these great cities consider their parks and greenways, and other great manmade public squares, to be essential. And many have excellent public transportation systems, which we strive to use for daily adventures, walking and taking in the wonderful sights, sounds, and exotic flavors. Through our travels, and experiencing the unique offerings and natural setting of world cities, I believe that I'm now better able to see what it is that makes Nashville great and what may make it great for future generations.

After World War II, in the United States, people began moving out of the urban centers to the proverbial tree-lined streets of the suburbs. Today people are moving back into the cities. This migration is important, as it gives us humans the chance to live more efficiently and to reduce our ecological footprint. It also creates more human connection, with important cultural benefits that impact our evolution. It requires that we become good stewards of our city and provide access to open space and public transportation, walkability, and a way to utilize the natural resources that our cities have to offer, like Nashville's Cumberland River with its nine bends. It's not important just to our city; it's important to the world. In Nashville, we have an opportunity and obligation to set an example and to show how this good stewardship will influence future leadership.

These conversations need to include the best transportation alternative: walking. People will walk to catch public transportation if it will reliably deliver them to their destination with a reasonable walk at the other end. In Jeff Speck's excellent book *Walkable City*, he suggests that there are ten keys to creating walkability. Most of these keys have something to do with redressing the deleterious effects of allowing cars to dominate urban spaces for decades. He also suggests that while walkability benefits from good transit, good transit relies absolutely on walkability.

Walking also has health benefits, and here in Nashville, where we have over three hundred health care companies, we should be thinking about "lean and green" as we continue to build out our greenways and focus on walkability and public transportation. Sherry and I love to walk, as do many of our neighbors. We each have a Fitbit and make a point off walking at least five miles per day, challenging each other to see who gets the most. For me, that means walking to work, having "walking" meetings with my agents and staff, walking phone calls, and lots of time on the greenways. Researchers now say that walking is the new wonder drug and prescribe thirty minutes of vigorous walking per day and even more for children. Side effects include weight loss, improved mood, and improved sleep. Biking and other physical activity can also do the trick, but the nice thing about walking is that it costs little or nothing. It is simple. It can be done by people of all ages, incomes, and fitness levels. And it is easier to stick to than other fitness prescriptions.

As you know if you read my fifty by fifty lists, I like to track things. Fitbit tracks walking and climbing for me and even gives me badges when I hit various achievements. I get the daily awards, like the Urban Boot, for fifteen thousand steps in a day (which I've now done 144 times), and the Skyscraper, which I got for climbing a hundred floors in a day (just once). I love it, and lifetime awards just come out of the blue. Like when, all of a sudden, my Fitbit notifies me that I have achieved the Great Barrier Reef award with "This reef is the world's largest coral reef system, and you just walked that." Or: "Whoa, you've walked the length of the Sahara Desert, which stretches from the Atlantic Ocean to the Red Sea." Or the Shooting Star: "You just climbed as high as a shooting star. So, make a big wish, and set a new goal." What we measure is what we do, and it might make sense for us to provide more measurement. I have heard that in Seoul, they pay people if they walk. That's an interesting health care initiative.

The 2013 Walking Summit, convened by Kaiser Permanente and the Everybody Walk! collaborative, focused on how to encourage more Americans to walk and how to make communities across the country more walkable. Scott Bricker, executive director of America Walks, a coalition of 470 organizations nationwide, joked that the ultimate goal was to make "sitting the new smoking." His ambitious vision for 2020 is that all Americans walk enough each day to enjoy health benefits and that all communities can provide a safe, comfortable environment for people to walk.

Karen Marlo, vice president of the National Business Group on Health, an alliance of leading companies, explained, "Walking is a business issue. A healthy workforce means a more successful workforce. It's important for businesses to share effective ways to get employees to walk more." The real estate developer Christopher Leinberger of LOCUS outlined how the rise of walkability is also good for our economic future. Every point over seventy on Walk Score results in increased rents of ninety cents per square foot for commercial property and a rise in home values of $20 per square foot for residential property. Harriet Tregoning, director of the Washington, D.C., Office of Planning, said, "What makes people walk is what makes great places to live. Walkability is the secret sauce that improves the performance of many other things."

And if you are not walking, how about a bicycle? Bicycling is the fastest growing form of transportation. In 2014, Americans bought more bikes (eighteen million) than they did cars and trucks combined (sixteen million). Active transportation is trending. In 2002, there were just seven bike share systems worldwide. Now there are 750 bike share systems worldwide, including 80 in the United States alone. In 2015, eighty-two US cities adopted complete street programs to accommodate cycling, bringing that number to nine hundred cities and towns in the United States that have now adopted these policies. In our travels to Amsterdam, Sherry and I were astounded at the number of people using bikes. Apparently, Amsterdam used to be like Nashville; they intentionally decided to create the biking infrastructure, and the people have adapted.

In cities where these systems and policies have been adopted, there is a surge in ridership. Biking is up 443 percent in Portland, Oregon, from 1990 to present, and now up 142 percent in Austin. As Nashville continues to lay down greenways, complete streets, and add to our B-Cycle stock, ridership in our city will increase. People bike for transportation and recreation but also for better health, to save money, and to run errands. If we make it easy and safe, people will walk or bike. In our master planning discussions for our Metro Park system, Plan to Play, greenways were cited as the number-one reason people used our parks, and walking and biking were cited as the two most preferred activities for health and recreation.

Biking infrastructure provides a lot of bang for the buck. Portland says that it created three hundred miles of complete streets and greenways for the cost of one mile of freeway. Structured parking costs a developer more than $20,000 per unit. A decent commuter bicycle costs somewhere between $300 and $1,000. A developer could provide a hundred bikes for the cost of two structured parking units. Some cities, like Vancouver, are reducing parking requirements in exchange for more bicycle infrastructure.

Sherry encourages the concept at LetterLogic, paying her people bonuses if they walk or bike to work. Hopefully there is a next level with healthy tracking tools such as Fitbit, so that we can promote the health and well-being of all residents in our city. This is where I call out our health care community of more than three hundred health care start-ups in our city, which collectively have a huge breadth of knowledge: Nashville is an epicenter of medical research, innovation, and entrepreneurship, but the city ranks poorly in terms of citizen health and levels of obesity, smoking, and hypertension. Support our greenways and walkability, create measurement and tracking tools, and contribute your expertise in the world of health here at home, in our community. And, in the spirit of our health care entrepreneurialism, you'll likely make money as you invent and then sell your wares to the many urban core communities throughout the United States.

Greenways and bikeways go hand in hand with public transportation, and greenways can act as transportation corridors. Additionally, it is now apparent that communities located near greenways are more desirable for home buyers. Greenways for Nashville (GfN) was founded in the mid-1990s by Mayor Bredesen's administration with the help of Charlie Tygard of the Metropolitan Council. The goal of this advocacy group is to create greenway access to all Nashville neighborhoods, to procure land for Nashville's park system, and to protect our wetland habitats. I got involved first as a volunteer and gave GfN memberships as closing gifts for my customers. In 2006 I was honored as the GfN Volunteer of the Year, having pledged over a thousand memberships to the new condo dwellers in downtown and midtown.

I was appointed to the mayor's Open Space Advisory Committee in 2007. This committee was charged with analyzing our greenways and park system. We reviewed the role that the Metropolitan Nashville Government, Metro Parks and Recreation and its Greenways Commission, and GfN had in implementing a long-term plan. As many fast-growing American cities do, Nashville needed a green strategy. The area's population had jumped by 10 percent in just a decade, while only 3 percent of Davidson County was devoted to parkland. Meanwhile, obesity-related conditions had cost area residents an estimated $255 million annually.

The website of the Conservation Fund, which worked with Land Trust for Tennessee to implement the plan, says it best:

> Located in Davidson County, Tennessee, Nashville is a uniquely beautiful place, defined by the wide and winding Cumberland River that flows through downtown, and surrounded by forested hills, sites rich in history, community gardens, parks and lakes. These are the things that draw residents, visitors and businesses to the area and compel them to stay.

The Open Space Committee work resulted in "Nashville: Naturally," a body of work that called for a major park system in each quadrant of the county. The four park systems included the Warner Parks in the southwest, which were essentially complete. Beaman Park and Bells Bend Park formed the northwest base in a fertile bend in the river. The plan recommended a third park system in northeast Nashville, along Stone's River, and a fourth in the southeast, on Mill Creek.

In 2008 I stepped out of my volunteer role at GfN and joined the board, a team that included some stalwart environmentalists such as Ann Tidwell and Anne Davis. I became president of the board in 2012 and still enjoy that role today. I was appointed in 2011 to the Greenways Commission, acting as an advisor to the Mayor's Office and the Metropolitan Council, and I continue to serve as a commissioner.

As *The Plan of Nashville* notes, great cities have great rivers. Ours flows through our city for over fifty miles. Working with the Cumberland River and the smaller river systems that wind through Davidson County, such as Harpeth River, Stone's River, and Mill Creek, the Nashville: Naturally plan called for a designated habitat corridor. This worked synergistically with the GfN plan and its goal of using the river system to connect neighborhoods. Mayor Dean and his administration followed the recommendations of the Nashville: Naturally plan and made historic and strategic acquisitions in the northeast, southeast, and northwest quadrants.

The northeast quadrant is a series of parks now ranging from the Stone's River Mansion to Taylor Farm. It addresses a bend in the Cumberland River along the Stone's River, and jumps the Cumberland into Shelby Park and Cornelia Fort, where a pedestrian bridge, built during the Purcell administration, links otherwise disconnected neighborhoods. It jumps the Cumberland River again into Peeler Park and Taylor Farm, where another bridge for pedestrians will need to be built at some time in the future. The resulting park system in this quadrant now has over 1,600 acres.

The Stone's River Mansion was the first strategic acquisition, and GfN rallied to raise private funds to supplement foundation and public monies in order to buy it. The Ravenwood property was next, decommissioning a two hundred-acre private golf course. At the other end of the system, Cornelia Fort, an old 120-acre airstrip, was acquired and land was added to Peeler Park and Taylor Farm. The Mo Lytle Farm, six hundred acres, had been on our minds for years as another necessary greenway route. Mo finally did the right thing, selling his farm to the Metropolitan Government. Nashville completed the Mo Lytle purchase in December 2012 with the help of the Conservation Fund, the Land Trust for Tennessee, and the Mayor's Office, which ultimately allocated the $10 million funding through the capital budget. GfN independently raised $250,500 to support the cause.

As we stood in the rain on the bluff overlooking the property, with Mayor Dean and Tommy Lynch of Metro Parks at the podium, the mayor cited the addition of the Lytle Farm to the greenways system as a "forever" opportunity. This was an amazing accomplishment and now had the added benefit of greening and connecting "hip" Donelson and other urban-ish neighborhoods to our urban neighborhoods in East Nashville. With another Cumberland River pedestrian bridge, Madison will also be accessible.

The Dean administration became a champion for a park system in one of the fastest growing, yet most economically challenged, sectors of the county. Southeast Nashville, with Mill Creek as the watershed, had significant flooding in the Great Flood of 2010. A lot of pavement in the southeast, which includes Antioch, made conditions ripe for flooding. GfN worked with the Dean administration and pieced together three hundred acres of land in this quadrant along Mill Creek.

In 2015, the final year of Dean's mayoral term, a 590-acre addition to the park was secured at the cost of $18.1 million with the help of the Joe C. Davis Foundation, on which Anne Davis, the mayor's wife and a GfN board member, serves as a trustee. The foundation committed $4.1 million in funding for this purchase. This quadrant is coming together, but it will still require some imagination and vision as well as "ripping up some asphalt," as my friend Gregor, the mayor of Vancouver, likes to say, turning parking lots into parks.

In the northwest, the Gilbert Forest in Beaman Park, a 568-acre park addition, was to be the last hurrah of the Dean administration. I attended the dedication, where Shain Dennison of Metro Parks and Jeanie Nelson of the Land Trust for Tennessee were honored by Mayor Dean for their work, which has created a park that now has over two thousand acres. What an astounding success! Nashville's four quadrants now each have a significant park system, as outlined in Nashville: Naturally.

Greening Nashville hasn't always been easy. As with any initiative, there have been pitfalls and challenges. In 2008, a proposal came up that worked against our greening efforts. While Mayor Dean and GfN were working to secure property for parks in the four quadrants, a 2008 proposition for the creation of a new 550-acre city center in Bell's Bend, called May Town Center, was on the table. May Town promised lots of residences and forty thousand jobs, and the developers were seeking rezoning. Bell's Bend is a rural bend in the Cumberland River where the May family had purchased nine hundred acres of land. This plan for intensive development required massive economic development incentives and a new bridge across the Cumberland River. This was certainly contrary to plans envisioned for Nashville, but it gained traction.

It seemed crazy that there was even a discussion. We had not even fully formed our own downtown, and yet we were considering a rival. Our city's planning manual creates what it calls transects, which describe the various development patterns of a region. They are T1 Natural, T2 Rural, T3 Suburban, T4 Urban, T5 Centers, T6 Core, and D Districts. The recommendation for the May Town Center was to put a T6 in the middle of a T2—that is, to put the most intensive zoning allowed in the middle of farmland. The zoning request was the most extreme possible and was diametrically opposed by the Scottsboro Community Plan, which described the area as a rural community that developed at a natural pace. While proponents embraced May Town Center as an opportunity to compete with Williamson County for corporate relocations, critics, led by Barry Sulkin, called the proposal harmful sprawl that would taint one of the county's environmental jewels.

As a developer, I am aware of the protocol that a developer does not publicly chastise another developer's project. I was looking at this with my open space stewardship hat on, but the community knows me better as a Realtor and a developer. As the lone developer in vocal opposition, I shared my views at a packed Metropolitan Planning Commission meeting. We were just beginning to realize the potential of our true urban core, and we knew our city did not need to lose focus. We were in a recessionary climate, and we needed to concentrate our efforts in the real city of Nashville. And I noted that Bell's Bend, with farmland close to the city, is a wonderful asset in this agrarian sector, which now best represents the farm-to-table movement.

The Metropolitan Planning Commission stalled the project in a rather bizarre 5–5 vote, which, because of this setback, meant that the project needed twenty-seven of forty votes to pass through the Metropolitan Council. The developers, of course, tried to blitz the Metropolitan Council members, but ultimately they failed. The hotly contested May Town Center, the Field of Dreams satellite city in bucolic Bells Bend that had divided Nashville like no other development issue in years, has now faded into the past.

Now that the May Town challenge was off the table, I felt like we might be in for a little bit of smooth sailing, but I was wrong! As chair of the ULI Sustainability Committee, I invited Sadhu Johnston, now the city manager of Vancouver, to come to Nashville for a ULI event that we dubbed "Sustainability as an Economic Engine." Sadhu gave us some great insights into public transportation and noted that one should put public transportation on the corridors and make sure that the stops are where people want to go. He also said a city should couple a public transportation system with rezoning initiatives, allowing for densification along the route, particularly near the major stops.

At the time, we were ramping up discussions about our public transportation system, and many of our city leaders, designers, and others in our ULI chapter were in attendance. On the panel were Ed Cole of the Transit Alliance; Jimmy Granbery from H.G. Hill, a supporter of public transportation and enhanced density; Laurel Creech from the Mayor's Office; and myself.

But the Amp, proposed as the first section of a Bus Rapid Transit System, met with stiff resistance, particularly from those who live and work on West End Avenue. There was a lot of concern about losing lanes that are currently used for automobile traffic, and herein lies the conflict. As Enrique Penalosa, the former mayor of Bogota says, "An advanced city is not a place where the poor move about in cars, rather it's where even the rich use public transportation." The opposition got out in front of the issue, and the project did not come to fruition. Perhaps it was a flawed initiative, but our city still needs a comprehensive plan. So, some of the challenges continue, but it helps to reach out to other communities for support and a yes-we-will attitude when facing local community naysayers. As Penalosa also notes, "Urban transport is a political and not a technical issue. The technical aspects are very simple. The difficult decisions relate to who is going to benefit from the models adopted."

Together Gregor, Sadhu, and their cohorts laid out a strategy in Vancouver and have been very aggressive in its implementation. Their transportation policy puts the car low in the hierarchy of transportation options. Pedestrians and bikers are on the top, so there has been an aggressive policy to give them priority. City streets have been decreased in width to allow for clear, separated bike lanes, and Vancouver now has a greenway around its entire seawall, where bikes and pedestrians have their own lanes. In the transportation hierarchy, cars are behind buses, trams, and other public transportation systems, including car-share programs. Cars are losing parking spaces to bike lanes and car share in the city core, and the city is gradually weaning itself off automobile transport.

Sadhu is now presiding over a group of more than a hundred sustainability directors in North America who work to share best practices so that cities can move smart initiatives forward with good strategy and use case studies from elsewhere for support. He has published a book titled *The Guide to Greening Cities,* which specifically addresses current issues, including public transportation issues, in the many cities that are getting into the act. When Nashville moved toward stewardship and sustainability as a community, we not only strengthened our own city but also joined a worldwide community of others looking to green up. That's how cities can change the world, one green-up effort at time.

NashvilleNext, the multiyear planning process conceived of during the Dean administration under the guidance of Rick Bernhardt, former planning director for Nashville, is a plan created for and by Nashvillians and is intended to serve as a guide to how and where we will grow in Nashville and Davidson County over the next twenty-five years. It is built on our community's goals and vision—ensuring opportunity for all, expanding accessibility, creating economic prosperity, fostering strong neighborhoods, improving education, championing the environment, and building on our unique strengths as a city. At the forefront of the concerns voiced by our citizens are preserving our neighborhoods while building housing close to transit and jobs; protecting rural character and natural resources; creating walkable centers; expanding walking, biking, and transit; and making our city affordable for all Nashvillians.

In sessions that I attended, where people used the "blue dot" system to define where they wanted to see more housing, the attendees overwhelmingly put their dots in emerging urban neighborhoods and on the major corridors. The people seemed to think that density on the corridors is a good thing and that this will create the type of housing that we need in order to further both walkability and access to affordable housing. However, the city is going to need some backbone as it goes through the zoning process to allow for the density on these corridors. Despite the fact that these corridors and emerging urban neighborhoods are the best places to allow for density, there is always pushback from neighbors, called NIMBYism (Not In My Back Yard), when the density being proposed is in their neighborhood. Indeed, in one neighborhood meeting I attended while proposing a Core Development project, I heard the comment "I believe in density on the corridors; just not here."

When Nashville's Chamber of Commerce delegation went to Vancouver in 2014, I was able to introduce Gregor and many of his key staff to our city leaders, including Mayor Dean and Anne Davis. Gregor hosted our first breakfast in the city and talked about his green mandate and some of the strides the city was making. We were particularly interested in Vancouver's transportation policies and systems and learned a lot that we hoped to bring back home.

The mayors Dean and Robertson had already met—well, sort of. When the Nashville Predators won a playoff spot in 2012 and successfully navigated to the second round, their opponent was the Vancouver Canucks. I reached out to both mayors and suggested a friendly mayoral bet. Mayor Dean rose to the occasion and issued the challenge. Dean said that if the Canucks beat the Predators, he'd gift Gregor a Tennessee smoked ham and ten CDs from our favorite local musicians. Robertson responded and told Karl that he was on and promised a Frasier River Smoked Salmon and ten CDs from favorite Vancouver artists if the Preds won. I was in Vancouver for two games and actually heard Mayor Dean on the radio, laying down his challenge. The Canucks won in six games, and Gregor won the spoils.

Given that our city kicked the Amp and our conversations about public transportation down the road during the Dean administration, it is good that Mayor Megan Barry was also on the trip. This has now become one of her signature issues, and she has revealed a $6 billion plan for the Nashville region, beginning with a light rail system on Gallatin Pike. Gregor is now serving a third term, thus perhaps we can continue to share best practices. Given that Vancouver is aiming to be the greenest city in the world, and that Nashville is the "It" city, we have a lot to share.

The transportation conversation, aside from the walking, biking, bus, and train options, now includes the autonomous vehicle and ride-sharing options like Uber and Lyft. In his book *Clean Disruption of Energy and Transportation*, Tony Seba calls the autonomous car the ultimate disruptive machine. The race to create these vehicles is on, and he believes that the movement will disrupt the oil and automobile industries, given that these cars will be electric and people will own fewer cars. Additionally, the switch to these vehicles will have the added bonus of saving lots of lives, given that they are better drivers than their human counterparts. These options may help with the "last mile" and may shift the way we look at highways and parking. We may soon see AV lanes on the highways, and many parking garages in the city may become obsolete.

Autonomous vehicles, for instance, are a lot "smarter" than human drivers and therefore take up less space on highways and roads and in parking garages. They do not have to circle forever to find a space—in fact, the autonomous vehicle and ride-sharing options do not require any parking from passengers in most instances. They are still both "cars," however, and should not be an excuse to kick the other public transportation options down the road. The only thing worse than a car on the road with just one occupant is a car with no occupants. We still need options, like buses and trains, that move people in bulk with regularity.

But the impact of autonomous vehicles will be felt far beyond what happens on the streets. The city experience that has relied on cars for the past century will swing toward a much more people-focused design. With less space for the 260 million cars, motorcycles, and buses on U.S. roads, bike lanes and sidewalks will be free for widening, leading to more space for pedestrians. Street-side parking lanes will be transformed into sidewalk cafés, and buildings will be reshaped, with the front door replacing the parking garage as the primary point of entry. This newly freed space will make way for amenities and mixed-use projects with apartments, offices, stores, and community gathering places, bringing new life to the already vibrant cityscape. We are beginning to think about these "road diets" on our inner Nashville corridors, noting that these pedestrian-friendly zones tend to be our most vibrant urban communities.

In Dean's last year as mayor, the West Riverfront Park opened. I thought a lot about the days of BURNT (Bring Urban Recycling to Nashville Today), when we were just trying to remove the downtown incinerator, and was so happy that we'd evolved this location into a 12.5-acre park system. This site almost became the Nashville Sounds' new ballpark back in 2008, with a couple hotels and a sixteen-story condo tower called Gateway, at the edge of the bridge, which I was to sell. In this instance, the economic slowdown saved an important property for a better use. Now, the park features an amphitheater that seats 6,500 people, and the grounds are animated with a beautiful sculpture made of steel, guitar picks, and LED lights. The immense structure's bends and curves reflect the shape of the nine bends in the Cumberland River as it winds through Davidson County.

An active Ascend Amphitheater. Photo courtesy of Aerial Innovations of Tennessee.

The park also provides a critical link to Nashville's greenways system, connecting two existing greenways through downtown—the Rolling Mill Hill greenway to the south and the MetroCenter Levee greenway to the north—a continuous paved trail more than twenty-five miles long. It also provides an easy connection between the Shelby Street Bridge, now the John Seigenthaler Pedestrian Bridge, and East Nashville. Though the full riverfront master plan has yet to be realized, Nashville has made great progress toward fully utilizing its urban river scene.

A ribbon cutting at one of the many new greenways added under Mayor Dean's watch.

As the plans for the Music City Center were unfolding, we were thinking about a downtown greenway loop that would connect the downtown riverfront parks, past Music City Center, with the Gulch, and go through the North Gulch across Charlotte, and then past the farmers' market, through Sulphur Dell, and back down to the river. An inner loop, we reasoned, would be good for future Music City conventioneers, for our Music City honky-tonk guests, for our downtown office workers, and for our emerging downtown residential community. If our city had this two- to three-mile inner loop, guests would have recreational access to key locations, and Nashville would be more interesting. A perfect loop would provide a walk/bike route, which would support the health and well-being of our city's inner residents.

This vision is now becoming a reality. The pending $18 million pedestrian bridge across the train tracks into the Gulch is the lynchpin, as it will connect the Gulch Greenway, which is a fabulous complete street through the Gulch, to the Music City Center and downtown. Capital View, a project that includes HCA's new subsidiary campus, plans a pocket park and greenway connector that will connect our inner loop to the Nashville Farmers' Market. From there, a walker/biker can get back to the river via a greenway that runs by the Nashville Sounds' new AAA ballpark. What guest or resident wouldn't want to make this scenic trek?

L: The John Seigenthaler Pedestrian Bridge, home to Dinner on the Bridge.
R: Mark and Sherry at Dinner on the Bridge.

It is evident that our downtown riverfront park system, with these amazing alternative transportation connections, is the backdrop that makes Nashville a great city. Greenways for Nashville celebrates our accomplishments each year with a "Dinner on the Bridge," a dinner with some 450 favorite friends on the John Seigenthaler Pedestrian Bridge. The city is a beautiful backdrop for the event, and in my first year as president I brought in the jugglers for our entertainment. Jacob Weiss and his troupe, Playing by Air, greeted the guests as they arrived with some juggling revelry, and I jumped in for a few throws as well.

Mark toasting Karl and Anne Davis.

At our annual event for GfN in 2015, unfortunately a "rain-out," at the Musicians Hall of Fame, I was honored to toast Mayor Karl Dean and Anne Davis. I complimented the mayor's many accomplishments during his administration, including the addition of 4,500 acres to our park system, a 25 percent increase, and the doubling of our paved greenway trails, from forty to eighty miles, and the creation of our downtown riverfront parks. I then asked the audience to consider the phrase "Behind every good man is a great woman," and proceeded to highlight the extraordinary environmental accomplishments of the mayor's wife, Anne, an attorney who ran the Nashville office of the Southern Environmental Law Center, an organization that protects our natural resources in the Southeast. She has been the quiet force at GfN, has had a hand in many of the strategic acquisitions, and is certainly the "great woman" behind an accomplished mayor.

Chapter 10

Urban Magnets

Nashville is the place we have made for ourselves. The strategies taken to make it a healthier place we must make for ourselves as well.

—Christine Kreyling,
The Plan Of Nashville

WHEN I WAS younger, on a walkabout, I used my juggling as a means to engage with people in other countries. Juggling is a fascinating tool that overcomes language and cultural barriers, and I love being the gringo who bears a gift. I would set up in a public square, juggle until the children gathered, and then engage with them. I would lay the kids on the square and juggle above them while they squirmed nervously. I could take several of them, moving them horizontally in a juggling like pattern, using them like juggling balls. I got behind them, put their hands in mine, and turned them into little jugglers. The parents loved it, and I created many relationships that led to camaraderie and offers for food and lodging with newly found friends. In some of these small towns in foreign lands, I would gain some celebrity, given the novelty of my offering.

In a northern Moroccan city I was swarmed with children and young teens as I juggled and quickly created a scene. I was an urban magnet. I had a sense that these kids were really keen, that they could see and even understand my moves as I juggled three, four, and even five balls. I did some teaching, and many of them immediately caught on. The soldiers in the square did not like the large gathering and dispersed the crowd, but over the course of a few days as I toured the town, I'd see my young students, who moved their hands to show that they recognized me as their juggling teacher. I saw the kids using my techniques to teach other kids to juggle, and a whole new tribe of jugglers emerged. I like to think that town now has bunches of great jugglers who have now studied and learned the craft!

Bringing people together in an urban setting continued as I worked in Nashville. And that bringing together turned into growth, as it so often does. Our city has become an urban magnet, attracting businesses and lots of people. It is estimated that the population in Nashville/Davidson County will gain 185,000 residents, and the region at least a million new residents, by 2040. Many, notably, will be immigrants from other parts of the world, which will require particular attention and focus—a bit of a juggle, you might say.

Nashville's downtown population is also skyrocketing, according to the NDP. It has spiked 40 percent since 2012 and topped 9,600 people by the end of 2016. It is poised to jump another 50 percent in the next two years, as many urban apartment developments complete. The demographic is shifting, and household incomes of 63 percent of downtown residents surveyed now top $100,000. Developers are accommodating this surging population, building high-end apartment buildings in all downtown neighborhoods. The emerging workforce is attracting a next round of office buildings, as businesses locate to suit their lifestyle preferences. The Nashville skyline is full of cranes, and with the *New York Times* giving us the moniker of "It" city, we have an opportunity to use our money and resources to shape our city's destiny.

What makes a magnet? When I think of Nashville's magnetic growth, I can't imagine that it would have occurred without a vital park system downtown on the Cumberland River. When I say "the core is the new edge," I imagine a vibrant downtown riverfront system, with parks and greenways across the city front on both sides of the river and greenways connecting to the neighborhood and park fabric in both directions. The riverfront has been designed and created to provide new public attractions, parkland, and waterfront access, giving residents and visitors the chance to enjoy both banks of the river. The East Cumberland Park, a 6.5-acre park under the Shelby Street Bridge on the east bank of the river, opened in 2012. The park has water features, including a water play park, climbing wall, ropes course, and an amphitheater with a wonderful backdrop of the city's fine skyline. A restored crane and a catwalk projecting over the river allow for viewing passing boats. The West Cumberland Park followed, and our riverfront system continues to develop.

With these many improvements in our city, tourist flow is also surging. Music City continues to command recognition with an influx of famous music and film stars and with the generally favored status of country music. The Music City Center, so well located, is big and attractive and brings all kinds of well-attended conventions with conventioneers who want to experience this southeast jewel of a city. New hotels are coming up all around the downtown, and room rates are purported to rival rates in New York City. As the residential, office, and tourist populations rise, urban retail is returning to the core—a renaissance of sorts, when one recalls the old days of Cain-Sloan and Castner Knott.

Nashville, the television show, has done wonders for our reputation, and the stars of that sitcom act as ambassadors for Nashville and its music. One of our Village agents, Barbara Moutenot, has sold a number of homes to the actors on the show as they continue to put down roots. One day, in late 2013, she was showing homes to Hayden Panettiere, who stars as Juliette Barnes on the show, and to her fiancé Wladimir Klitschko, then the twelve-year reigning world heavyweight boxing champ. I was holding an open house on a new build in the Hillsboro Village when they dropped in.

Given that the open house was on our street, Sherry happened to drive by as they were getting out of the car, saw them, and sent me a text saying, "I bet you're happy." She was referring to Hayden, of course, knowing that I'm a big fan of the show. The couple liked the finishes and the work of the builder, but the home was not quite the right fit. As it goes, Sherry and I had visited with Brent Craig, the builder, on that very morning, and he'd shown us what was going to be his personal home, which he had just completed. But he was also open to selling the home. I let Barbara know, and as the final negotiations were taking place, Brent said that he'd take the couple's final offer if Wladimir would provide ringside seats to his next fight. Great negotiation, and the deal was sealed.

In April of 2014, Brent and I flew to Oberhausen, Germany, for the fight. It was an amazing experience, an international scene complete with Wladimir's Ukrainian entourage and Hayden's devotees. Who knew that Hayden was such a boxing fan! We were ringside when Wladimir defeated his opponent in a fifth-round knockout, one of his last professional victories before his retirement.

Perhaps nothing defines an urban magnet better than a thriving arts scene. After the final Werthan Mills Lofts were sold, Core Development was looking for the next big thing. In 2014 we decided to focus its efforts in Wedgewood Houston, an up-and-coming neighborhood within Nashville's urban revitalization narrative. As one of the last urban ring neighborhoods, Wedgewood Houston is located squarely at the nexus of I-65 and I-40, within close proximity to the

Gulch, Edgehill Village, Hillsboro Village, and 12South. Inspired by Wedgewood Houston's prevailing "maker" movement and art scene, Core announced plans to develop Nashville's first live/make community, calling our project The Finery.

The neighborhood culture is defined by the makers and artists. Fort Houston, just up the block, has ten thousand square feet, complete with a full-scale wood shop, print shop, bike shop, photography studio, and miscellaneous work and desk spaces. Fort Houston, which bills itself as a place for people to facilitate, grow, learn, and work, is membership based, and members have the use of shared facilities and training. Wedgewood Houston (nicknamed WeHo) has long been a neighborhood driven by strong artisan relationships and has functioned as a historic home for many artist studios. Every month, there is a free art and music walk. To coincide with Art Night in Nashville, the walk begins at 6 p.m. on the first Saturday with dozens of venues, commercial galleries, artist-run studios, and coworking spaces exhibiting groundbreaking art.

With over nine acres of land secured in the heart of this neighborhood, Core Development ultimately had the property rezoned for 490 residential units, eighty thousand square feet of commercial (maker) space, and twenty-five thousand square feet for restaurants. Our hope was that the retail and light industrial/artisanal spaces would complement existing enterprises within the neighborhood that included music production studios, art galleries, vintage motorcycle repair shops, organic coffee roasting facilities, handmade skateboard makers, furniture builders, and more. Among the other more notable enterprises located in Wedgewood Houston are Gabby's Burgers, United Record Pressing, Houston Station, the Clean Plate Club, and Zeitgeist Gallery. The area has witnessed numerous business announcements that include David

Lusk Gallery, Smokin Thighs, Dozen Bakery, Clawson's Pub & Deli, Bastion, and the new food court St. Roch Nashville.

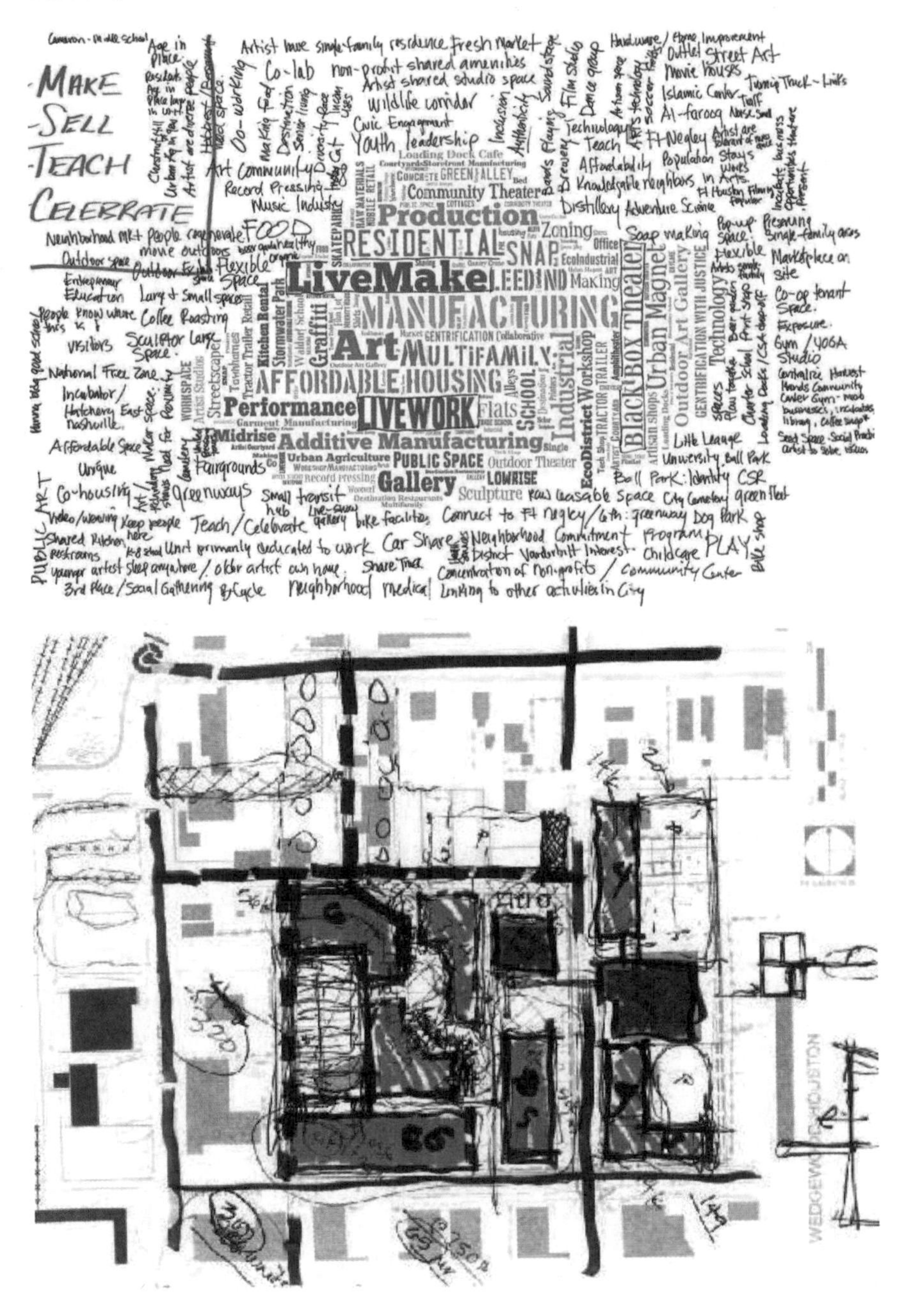

Prior to rezoning the property, we held a charrette. We invited neighborhood leaders, business owners, and members from the Nashville Metro Planning Department to help us with a master plan. What resulted was interesting, and the live/make community concept evolved. The Planning Department and neighbors asked us to consider creating more density with our projects and felt that buildings of four to six stories were the appropriate height, given that our project sat in a bowl, twenty to thirty feet lower than the surrounding streets. This density and height, and our location just one mile from the Music City Center, allowed us to consider skyline views.

The neighbors had a vision for their community and were very pointed in their recommendations. They wanted affordable housing, mixed-use zoning, and walkable services, and therefore actually wanted more density. They wanted our project to serve the makers and artists in the community. All of this became a part of our Special Plan (SP), which now guides our series of developments. We noted in the process that "density is not necessarily our friend." By building higher-density, mixed-use condominiums in a real estate environment that has been mostly devoid of condos post-recession, there is more development risk, but we agreed that this was a better plan.

I'd been inspired in this by another thriving urban community that featured crafts, education, industrial, retail, and housing, and which epitomized the concept of what a city core can be: Granville Island in Vancouver, British Columbia. The firm of Alan Boniface, an architect from Vancouver, was involved in the evolution of this vibrant mix of uses that has actually earned Granville Island the moniker of "urban magnet." Alan is a leading thinker on urban issues, is actively involved in the ULI Vancouver, and is one of the founders of a group called Urban Magnets.

MAKE
SELL
TEACH
LiveMake
Art
Gallery

Urban magnets are described as unique urban places that attract and hold activity groups, which animate a place and give it vitality, a sense of place, and economic success. The theory is that land use and design approaches can appeal deeply to a small, activity-oriented niche group, who then, by "living out loud," create an animated place that the rest of us (and many businesses) gather around to keep animated. Urban Magnet Theory, as espoused by this group, is dedicated to better the understanding of how to create these magnetic places.

I subscribe fully to this theory. The Nashville chapter of the ULI decided to create an Urban Magnet Committee, and Andrew Beaird, VP at Core Development, launched the committee as a co-chair. Andrew, an urban planner we recruited from Vancouver, had worked with Alan as a land planning consultant and invited him to keynote an event in Nashville, pairing him with a panel that included Rick Bernhardt.

Alan spoke to us about the components of a true urban magnet. He let us know that the foundation of any magnet is an activity and the group that engages in it enthusiastically. Furthermore, retail associated with the activity needs to be provided, and production space directly related to creating what is sold, or associated with the activity, is important. Educational uses also need to be included to bring employment and students into the space, creating an atmosphere of learning and exploration. Finally, there need to be programmed events. The urban form should be designed to respond to the identity and aesthetics of the activity subculture group at the heart of the urban magnet and needs to support the gathering of the people who wish to engage.

This committee hosted several subsequent events, including one at Zeitgeist, an art gallery, to see if Wedgewood Houston might have the potential to be an urban magnet. We will see how the neighborhood evolves, and hope that the maker subculture continues to thrive, even with the recent announcement that Fort Houston is relocating to a larger space in Melrose. Core Development was attracted to Wedgewood Houston when we recognized these characteristics and will work to develop what seems to be the geographical heart of the neighborhood. Our first two projects are Six10 Merritt and Twelve60 Martin. We are adding retail, live/work, and live/make spaces in our developments and hope to nurture more of what already exists. We have already attracted Bongo Java, and an urban market called Sassafras, in the Six10 and have various artists staking their claim to the live/make spaces at Twelve60.

It is super exciting to be working in a new neighborhood, and the energy is palpable. Darek Bell, who is in my Entrepreneurs' Organization forum, Forum 12, has decided to stake a claim in the neighborhood, expanding his operations with Corsair Artisan Distillery. Darek is interested in adding a distillery district to the neighborhood mix, and it appears that this is becoming reality, as the Nashville Craft Distillery has now opened. We sold an out-parcel to Adam Diskin, and Diskin Cider has announced. These distilleries support the craft maker culture with creation of fine spirits and add to the vibe of the district with tasting rooms and outdoor areas that face the street.

Max Goldberg, also in my EO forum, and cofounder with his brother Benjamin of notable restaurants such as Pinewood Social and The Catbird Seat, has entered the neighborhood with a restaurant at Houston Station, called Bastion, and has other concepts underway. Band members from Kings of Leon, who have their studio in the neighborhood, worked with Village agent Barbara Moutenot and purchased a number of properties. Their acquisitions include the Merritt Mansion, saving that site from a developer with less than inspirational intentions and perhaps adding another boutique hotel or foodie mix into the neighborhood equation. And now that T-Bone Burnett, the acclaimed musician/writer/producer and the original executive music director for the TV series *Nashville* and his development team have won their bid to redevelop the Greer Stadium site, with plans to focus on the artists and makers, the neighborhood has the potential to evolve into an urban magnet. With everything that is happening, the neighborhood has the potential to evolve into an urban magnet.

Urban magnets are kin to my concepts and work in that "one-mile radius." They have similar attributes. And part of what makes an urban magnet is what I've tried to advocate all along: walkability, better public transportation, and greenways. Nashville has a number of emerging opportunities, including urban transit- and trail-oriented development. In 2016, the ULI created a study entitled *Active Transportation and Real Estate: The Next Frontier,* authored by Ed McMahon (my muse for Go Green), which highlighted these emerging trends. Physical activity, once part of our normal lives, has for years been designed out of our daily routines. As Tim Gill, the founder of Rethinking Childhood, says, "Humans are disappearing from the outdoors at a rate that would make them top any conservationist's list of endangered species."

But individuals are likely to be more active in a community designed around their needs. Successful cities put people first. If we design around cars, there will be more cars. If we design around people, there will be more people. Designing around people makes us healthy, wealthy, more environmentally friendly. It makes us an urban magnet.

Across the globe, developers are seizing a competitive advantage by leveraging growing interest in biking and walking among residents along these corridors. Investment in infrastructure for walking and biking is called trail-oriented development. Past investment in roads and highways led to auto-oriented development; investment in public transportation leads to transit-oriented development. Likewise, investment in infrastructure for walking and biking leads to trail-oriented development.

Nashville has already been planning the beginning of what might become a trail-oriented development opportunity, and I believe this initiative could be one of the most important ways we can become an urban magnet. While the city was engaged in a very public conversation about the Amp, our failed first round in the evolving conversation about public transportation, some of us worked behind the scenes to implement an alternative transportation corridor. The 440 Greenway, as conceived, will use the interstate infrastructure to connect six arterial streets, connecting Franklin Road to Charlotte Pike, while crossing Granny White, Belmont Boulevard, Hillsboro Road, and West End Avenue.

The original plans for Interstate 440 had featured this greenway connector, but value engineering and the NIMBYs killed it. At the time, over thirty years ago, there was resistance to greenways in proximity to homes because we did not realize how valuable greenways are to our communities. This fight was similar to the resistance GfN faced when trying to connect river systems. If private property was involved, neighbors would come out in force to rally against them, citing crime and devalued properties. So much has changed today; all of the members of the Metropolitan Council are clamoring for a greenway in their district.

Tim Netsch, the assistant director of Metropolitan Parks and Recreation, shared with me a potential route for the 440 Greenway that he had mapped. I became an advocate, briefed the greenways commissioners, and enlisted support from the GfN board. I presented the route as an integral part of a public transportation plan that is relatively inexpensive, with potential to yield great results. I could also see that the 440 Greenway could provide the connection for a bigger bike/pedestrian loop around our city, one that created an alternative transportation corridor.

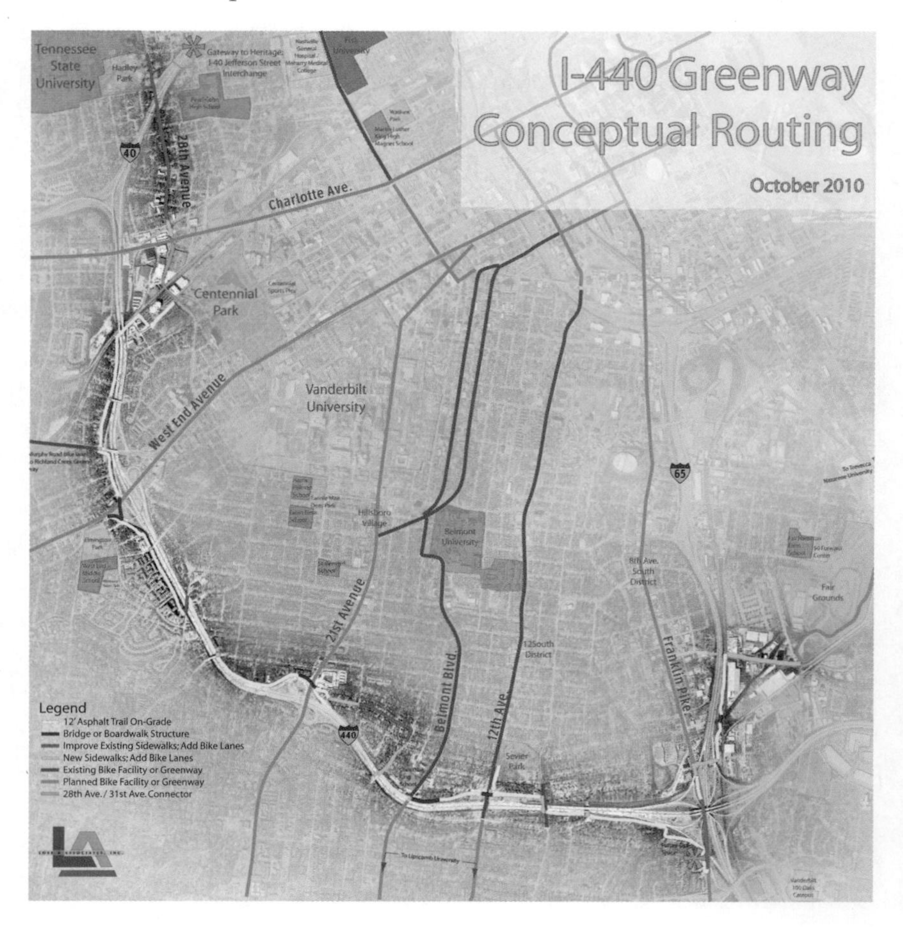

Much of the 440 Greenway route is pretty easy, given that the Tennessee Department of Transportation (TDOT) owns land adjacent to the interstate. Burkley Allen, the councilwoman for District 18, former councilman Jason Holleman of District 24, and I had a visit with Toks Omishakin, deputy commissioner at TDOT. Toks and his colleagues expressed a willingness to grant easements on TDOT land, or to turn the land over to Metro Parks and Recreation, and he encouraged us to get support from the Mayor's Office. In some places, however, there will be pinch points, and my hope is that some sections will be "inside the wall"—elevated sections of the greenway visible to passing cars on the interstate. That would be sexy, particularly when traffic is stalled, watching cyclists whizzing by overhead.

Mayor Dean and the Metropolitan Council funded the first section, from West End at Elmington Park to the Twenty-Eighth/Thirty-First Avenue Connector and Centennial Park in his final, 2015 capital budget. Additionally, the administration expressed support for an extension of the greenway up Twenty-Eighth Avenue N. to Hadley Park near Tennessee State University. This would create a greenway connector to an underserved neighborhood and could then be connected to the Ted Rhodes Greenway trailhead, which connects via Metro Center to the downtown riverfront. This, of course, means that a cyclist will soon be able to ride from all corridors along the 440 Greenway to downtown.

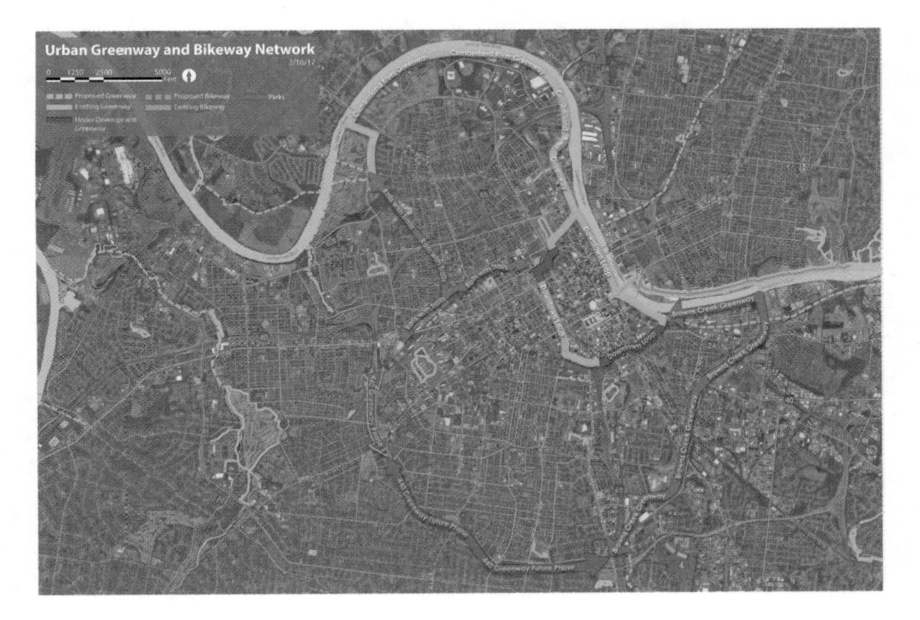

Browns Creek runs under the 440 Interstate at Franklin Road, and emerges behind the Melrose post office. GfN, with funding from the Village Fund, has mapped out how a Browns Creek Greenway would connect the 440 Greenway to connect to the Fairgrounds, then across Nolensville Road, to Murfreesboro Road at Trevecca, and finally to Hermitage Avenue and into the Cumberland River. We enlisted Collier Engineering for this study, which recommended a route that could use a complete street connector at Visco Drive that intersects with Browns Creek near Hermitage Avenue, to connect the Browns Creek Greenway to Rolling Mill Hill, and hence back to our downtown riverfront park system.

The 440 Greenway, and the bigger, twenty-five-mile loop, will create an alternative transportation system and some quick wins for our city as we embark on an ambitious public and active transportation plan. Sherry calls it the BassLine in honor of Music City. ("It's all about that bass, 'bout that bass, no treble," sings Meghan Trainor.) I like the name, as it mimics some other well-known greenways, like the High Line in NYC and the BeltLine in Atlanta. I presented this information to Gary Gaston of the NCDC, along with the concept of creating the big loop. The NCDC has included this information in its 2015 publication, *Shaping the Healthy Community*, authored by Gary Gaston, who is the organization's executive director, and Christine Kreyling.

I then shared these maps and concepts with Mayor Barry, who immediately took up the charge. The Mayor's Office, working with Adams Carroll, former Active Mobility Planner at Metropolitan Nashville–Davidson County Planning Department, and with Shain Dennison and Emmie Thomas at GfN, rallied and in late 2016 submitted a request for a $30 million TIGER Grant. TIGER (Transportation Investment Generating Economic Recovery) Grants have been available through the US Department of Transportation and fund capital investments that will have a significant impact on the nation, a metropolitan area, or a region. The program focuses on projects that generate economic development and improve access to reliable, safe, and affordable transportation for communities.

Though we did not get the grant in our 2016 submission, we made the final cut and got some great feedback for our resubmission. We think that we have a good shot at the grant in 2017, if the TIGER Grant program is continued, and it has become a rallying cry to raise private money for greenways. I have volunteered to raise $1 million privately, had raised $630,000 by the time the first grant request was submitted, and will work with GfN and the ULI to raise more funding from private sources. In the meantime, we have funding for a next section allocated in the 2016 capital budget and are actively planning to connect the next section of the 440 Greenway from Granny White to Franklin Road. Additionally, we received funding in 2017 for a one-mile section of the Browns Creek greenway.

With the first phase of the 440 Greenway under way, we invited our favorite ULI senior fellow, Ed McMahon, to keynote an event. Ed shared some amazing information about other urban trail-oriented development opportunities and results. He cited results from catalytic bike/ped programs in other cities and noted that there are over 1,700 miles of trail projects underway in the United States and 22,000 miles of trails already completed.

The BeltLine in Atlanta will be twenty-two miles long when complete and will connect forty-five neighborhoods. Four trail segments and six new parks are now open, and it is already considered a game changer in a city known for sprawl and traffic congestion. It is already spurring the redevelopment of three thousand acres of underdeveloped real estate, an estimated $1 billion of development next to the trail. The Midtown Greenway in Minneapolis has been dubbed the nation's first bike freeway, with separate lanes for bikes and pedestrians. At a cost of $36 million, this 5.7-mile-long greenway features bike stations and trailside cafes, making it a true urban magnet. It currently attracts over 5,300 cyclists per day and has spurred $750 million of mixed-use residential development. The Cultural Trail in Indianapolis, at 8.5 miles in length, connects six cultural districts, cost $63 million to develop, and has generated an estimated $864 million in economic impact with the creation of 11,300 jobs since it opened in 2008. These projects have the potential to catalyze an urban magnet.

Developers are creating bike-friendly projects, with wider hallways, bike storage, bike washing stations, bike workrooms, and showers in commercial buildings. Bici Flats in Des Moines, Iowa, has a bike valet service. Via6 in Seattle, a twenty-four-story building with 650 units, boasts that 70 percent of its residents no longer have a car. Developers note that their tenants pay rental premiums for these unique features and are marketing active transportation as an asset. Plus, these residents are healthier. It is estimated that the resident who lives in this type of environment weighs six to ten pounds less than their suburban counterpart. And because they do not have to endure the commute, they get more time with their community. To top it off, they are saving money, given that transportation is the second biggest household expense.

There are others: The Circuit in Philadelphia, currently at three hundred miles and counting, The 606 in Chicago, a 2.7-mile rail to trail completed in 2015 by the Trust for Public Lands, and the Cross-Charlotte Trail in Charlotte, which will be twenty-six miles long. I sat with Jim Garges, the head of parks and greenways in Charlotte, who informed me that the 1.5-mile urban section of the Little Sugar

Creek Greenway, with its many pocket parks, has already generated $367 million in economic development. In Charlotte, they call it "greenway-oriented development" (GOD). In a follow-up note, Jim said, "Let me show you how GOD works here." Downtown mixed-use projects along these trails create more jobs per acre, more taxes per acre, more residents per acre, and more people walking from their homes to retail and restaurants.

These retail services benefit from the multimodal access. When places that are accessible by foot or by bike capture people's affection, the people tend to stay longer, to come back more often, and to spend more money. Most of these urban trail-oriented developments give people three or four options for getting to a place, versus one—the car—for suburban retail locations. And demand for walkable, mixed-use design far outstrips supply. In all thirty of the largest metro areas the majority of all real estate development is occurring in walkable urban neighborhoods.

When Ed finished his presentation, I led a local panel, using Browns Creek as our case study. Shain Dennison shared the broad vision for the greater loop. Councilman Colby Sledge talked about upgrades to the Fairgrounds, including new soccer fields and a park system. David Caldwell, CFO of Trevecca, talked about how his campus, which abuts Browns Creek, can take advantage of this asset for their students. Britnie Turner, CEO of Aerial Development, shared her experiences with a trail-oriented residential development concept called East Greenway Park. It was an extraordinary event, and more than two hundred ULI members were educated and inducted into the local campaign.

The Browns Creek Greenway, when coupled with the 440 Greenway, has the potential to have catalytic impact in Nashville. Connecting the Melrose retail district to the Fairgrounds and Nolensville

Road, for instance, has potential to create an urban magnet, and trail-oriented development opportunities abound. Two strong mixed-use and retail districts will merge, and new neighborhoods will emerge. Nolensville Road boasts a diverse international community, and with the help of Conexión Américas and Casa Azafrán we will enhance Nashville's experience with the growing Hispanic community.

Core Development, with our mission now to further the creation of urban magnets, is launching a "trail-oriented development." We have contracted five acres on Tech Hill, over Browns Creek and the Fairgrounds, and another five acres next to the Fairgrounds. We believe that this location, which includes the Fairgrounds, is on the verge of being transformed, and that Browns Creek, as part of the emerging greenway system, is ripe for a reset at the intersection of Nolensville Road, particularly now that the proposition of a major-league soccer stadium is in the mix. We think the Fairgrounds will then connect with a greenway to the former Greer Stadium/Fort Negley park, and then down to the Music City Center. Tommy Lynch, quoting Shain Dennison in a retirement speech to the GfN board, noted that they will be "pearls of parks strung with greenways."

Tech Hill is already wrapped with Google Fiber, and the Nashville Technology Council has moved to their new office location, which is full of other young techies. Our first project is called Alloy, with eighty-two condominiums (forty of which are selling for under $200,000), twenty live/work units, and six light industrial units. We have attracted Bongo Java Roasting Company to the site. The Nolensville corridor is rich with diversity, and the Hispanic and Kurdish cultures, among other immigrant communities, are making their impact. The educational component of an urban magnet already exists at Casa Azafrán, under the stewardship of Renata Soto and her team.

I believe that other urban magnets will arise as we pursue densification on the corridors, and as we continue to develop our downtown riverfront, noted in the plan outlined by NashvilleNext. The Nashville Civic Design Center showcased a design contest for the PSC Metals plant, and eventually it will move from downtown Nashville. The East Bank north of Nissan Stadium has a significant development proposal on the books. And the Mayor's Office is looking for a "Teacher's Village," a place that nurtures those in our educational system and could anchor an urban magnet. Densification, affordable housing, and public transportation can go hand in hand, as developers use the tools that are being created to create places for our workforce and artists.

Here in Nashville, Music City, I want to remember and remind myself of the magnetism of the music scene, the underlying fabric of our city. At an event in early 2017, Sherry and I attended a screening for the television show *Nashville*, hosted by Mayor Barry to showcase her cameo appearance in the drama. In the crowd, I saw T-Bone Burnett, noted musician and original executive music producer for the TV drama, and recalled showing him homes years back. As I unlocked the door to enter one of the homes he was viewing, a dog attacked and bit my leg. T-Bone never bought a home from me, but that image is a good souvenir. Additionally, Sherry and I recently attended an event for Savannah Welch, an actress and musician who had lost her leg in a runaway car accident. Her dad, Kevin Welch, a notable singer/songwriter, had put together a benefit to honor his daughter, complete with his old band, the Dead Reckoners. The crowd was wonderful, and the concert was moving. I saw so many friends and former customers—and even Village agent Beth Hooker—on stage and in the crowd and was moved to tears at this outpouring of community fellowship. Sherry noted that this is why she loves Nashville and why Nashville is such a great city.

The transportation landscape is changing, and our city continues to invest in alternative transportation infrastructure, which will allow us to continue to be a magnet. Mobility sharing and autonomous vehicles will have a big impact. Bicycle and pedestrian infrastructure is catalyzing economic investment just as other forms of infrastructure have done in the past. Nashville is arguably behind our peer cities in a comprehensive active transportation system, but I believe that we can forge public/private partnerships here in Nashville to complete the BassLine (or whatever it is ultimately named!) with the resultant diversity of benefits realized, including health, economic development, and traffic relief. It will reverberate across the community to benefit our citizens and visitors. We are on our way.

Conclusion

Activism is my rent for
living on this planet.

—Alice Walker

WHEN I STARTED Village Real Estate Services in 1996, we were just two agents, two administrative staff members, and me. We now have over 350 agents and staff members, a strong team at Core Development, and a number of effective partnerships. Though we would not be considered a fast-growth company, we've had a notable progression, and I feel that Village is well positioned for the future. Core Development is an important factor in this growth, as it has leveraged our real estate sales and marketing company into an investment and development company. Our social purpose is now poised for immense new value with the vibrancy of the Village Fund and with the work that we are doing to nurture our Change Agents.

I like to think of Village and its goals as a machine whose flywheel keeps it balanced and ready to sustain itself for the long haul. In reading *Good to Great: Why Some Companies Make the Leap . . . and Others Don't* by Jim Collins, I was struck by the fact that many of our great companies had humble beginnings. They were not always great big companies, and many started locally, working to perfect their craft, before going big. As Collins noted, sometimes these companies kept their nose to the grindstone, turning the flywheel until such time as the bigger opportunity arose. The fact that many of these companies had ten or twenty years behind them before they made the move is inspiring. Many of them worked within their natural rhythm—with quarterly and yearly planning, goals and objectives, mission and purpose—to be the best that they could be. Most had no early intention of growing beyond their bounds, and their subsequent expansion was an evolution.

At Village, the flywheel has been steadily turning since 1996. We follow the Rockefeller Habits, a system outlined in a book of the same name by Verne Harnish, and work with Elizabeth Crook, our strategic planner and partner, trained in Verne's work, to set the company rhythm and energy. The quarterly planning process always starts with our mission and purpose, and we read these out loud. We remind ourselves what we are best at, and we always share successes from the previous quarter. We make sure to check in to see that our BHAG, or "Big Hairy Audacious Goal," is still relevant.

Generally, we look for and tackle one major initiative and then look to find four or five things that must get done in the following quarter. We then assign one person to drive the task. In this way, we weed out what is less important, keep our eye on the prize, and make sure that someone takes responsibility to reach our goals. I am always amazed at our quarterly successes and how much we get done. We also bring these major initiatives to the table at our weekly executive meetings and make sure that what we are doing is aligned with these bigger goals. In this way, the flywheel keeps turning and our company progresses in a meaningful way.

Our major goal, or BHAG, now at Village is to get to one thousand agents while continuing to focus on the city's core neighborhoods. Our BHAG at Core is to create twenty-five urban magnets. Additionally, I am looking to create a version of an Employee Stock Option Plan (ESOP) with Village, Core Development, and the City-Living Team, allowing top agents and staff to buy in to our continued success. These goals are a long-term investment in the "local living economy," but still offer the possibility that growth could take us elsewhere, as there are many cities that might be ready to receive a company like Village, or even Core Development. I have a great, diverse team with a lot of collective energy and experience, and their goals are likely bigger than mine, given that I am continually content with our work within a one-mile radius.

Juggling is, perhaps, still the most apt metaphor for the work I do today. Though I am not physically the juggler that I used to be, I have become more adept through the years. I often think of the various projects I tackle as balls in the air and use that focus and precision not to drop a ball. People comment that I seem to be able to track and do a lot with seemingly little effort. My wife, in particular, says that she works a lot harder than I do. This is partially true because I am a good collaborator and delegator, but it also has something to do with my facility at making the many moves needed to establish a good pattern while simultaneously making many small adjustments to keep things on track and moving forward. It's always better to make a lot of subtle moves, with the fluidity of a five-ball pattern, than to drop a bowling ball or machete into the mix.

Juggling has also taught me how to pick myself up off the floor. A juggler has to learn to deal with the drops, and the best jugglers are able to retrieve a dropped ball with a great move and, perhaps, a good pick-up line for the crowd. Dropping is just part of the act and is certainly part of life in the real (estate) world. A salesperson has daily ups and downs, as I did when I started out in the biz. It is essential that you let go of the small failures so that you are available for the big successes.

As a developer or community builder, you must be able to work together with others in the troupe, adapting your routine to each move or any mistakes you make as well as adjusting your performance to best serve others. Sometimes you have to pick up the slack for others, and sometimes you can just get out of the way and allow for another's special skills to carry the day.

I encourage my agents to have a unique selling proposition, USP, like a juggler with a unique shtick, something that differentiates them from all other agents in the community. This is their act, the thing that makes what they do stand out in the crowd. And like the best jugglers busking on the street, the agents with the best show get the best hats, making more money than their peers and doing the most for their community in the process. It's an apt metaphor for all of us, in our careers and in our lives. We are all jugglers, we all have our act, we all work and refine our patterns, and we all have to learn to drop.

I am still a juggler, though my act has shifted over time. I no longer juggle the "danger" items like fire and machetes, and I now only occasionally pass clubs with partners. I've certainly lost some of the dexterity of my youth, and the act must adapt to an aging body. In 2016, I was asked to "Dance for Safe Haven," a local version of "Dancing with the Stars," and was paired with a professional dancer, Juanita Simanekova. Juanita choreographed a fantastic dance for us with some jitterbug, Charleston, and swing, which we performed for a large audience in competition with five other couples, raising a bunch of money for the organization. Juanita managed to add a few bars of juggling into the routine, which wowed the crowd and reminded my audience that I still have some chops.

Our lives continue to evolve, and in the latter half of 2016 Sherry sold her company. For ten years straight, LetterLogic was on the *Inc.* 5000 list of fast-growth companies, which attracted a lot of attention and many unsolicited offers. The company's culture, fast growth, recurring revenue stream, and specialized niche in the health care industry were especially attractive. Sherry and her team decided to be intentional about grooming the company for sale. Ultimately, she sold to a venture capital group that paired her with a friendly competitor. The other company in the pairing had a great technology platform, and LetterLogic excels in printing and mailing statements—seemingly a good fit. Sherry has retained an investment position in the new venture, has a seat on the board, and hopes to be "the tail that wags the dog," as they talked about back at SVN, sharing best practices and wisdom from her years at the helm.

Sherry, true to her word, gave over 15 percent of the proceeds to her employees, and everyone who wanted it still has a job. Most pleasing were the conversations she had with the workers on the factory floor, who were compensated based on tenure. She would sit with them and say, for instance, "What would you do if you had a check for $30,000?" Some of these employees had come from hard times, some even from Safe Haven, and she wanted to share financial wisdom. When they answered responsibly, she gave them the check. Many have written back now telling her how her generosity has changed their lives. Some have paid off debt, some have done things for their families, and one has already left the company to pursue an entrepreneurial dream!

At the end of 2016, Joel and Dana visited Sherry and me at our house in San Miguel de Allende in Mexico. Sherry and I had purchased the home that year in the romantic location where we had gotten engaged. It is perhaps serendipitous that we convened at this time, given my history with Joel, the pull and connection that I still have from and with British Columbia, and the work that we do with our spouses. Joel, now a dual citizen, with his new book, *The Clean Money Revolution: Reinventing Power, Purpose, and Capitalism,* to be published in early 2017—perhaps perfect timing given the shift in Canadian and US politics, with the liberal Justin Trudeau upsetting his conservative opponent to become prime minister and after the conservative upset in the presidential race in the states. And Dana, announcing in late 2016 that she is stepping down as the executive director of Hollyhock after 2017, to focus her energy on raising money for the "Forever Fund," the endowment that will ensure the longevity of Hollyhock as a premier educational institution. And Sherry, with a company sale under her belt, underway with her new book, *SQS, The Status Quo Sux*, and readying for a busy year of speaking engagements and board work. And me, with this book, having furthered the work at Village and Core, while making some shifts in the stewardship and ownership of the organizations. As Joel likes to say, it is important to "elder early," to impart the wisdom of experience while the getting/giving is good.

Nashville and I have both come a long way over the last thirty years. In a way, you could say we have grown closer together as I've become a better steward, strengthening the one-mile radius concept to improve our neighborhoods and thereby deepening our relationship. I've learned that we are better together—that working together in partnership, respecting the diversity of opinions and backgrounds, and supporting nonprofits that do specific community work are important components in the creation of a healthy city. My particular work—selling lots of homes to good people, building out the greenway system, enhancing the park system, creating connectivity and walkable communities, retrofitting for energy savings, reusing existing infrastructure, creating attainable housing, densifying our corridors, and strengthening our alternative transportation system—has been important, but it is just one piece of the puzzle. From breathing new life into communities with developments such as Werthan Mills Lofts in Germantown and The Finery in Wedgewood Houston, to creating a community of Change Agents who give back through the Village Fund, I have done my best, with what I knew then and what I know now, to leave our city a little better than I found it all those years ago. I hope that you will join me and use your unique gifts to do good work in your one-mile radius.

Acknowledgments

I WOULD LIKE to thank those who have contributed to my education through the years and to those who have actively participated in the creation of this book. When I arrived in Nashville, I was very green, and I'm not talking "Go Green." I had a lot of street smarts from years of travel, and a few university degrees, but little in the way of practical work experience. I did not have a good sense of what community building really meant or what socially responsive business might look like. I was not in a position to make an impact in a "one-mile radius," but I had street smarts and an entrepreneurial spirit, and gradually and over time I found my place in Nashville, my home.

Over the years, many people have contributed to my continuing education, which is ongoing. Beginning in the Homewood House, to the "adults" who tolerated the teens as we experimented with collective living. Early mentors included Joel Solomon, my friend who first introduced me to Nashville neighborhoods, and Martha Burton, who worked with Joel and tried to instill skills like contract writing and attention to details. I learned early from friends at the Social Venture Network, like Gary Hirshberg, Judy Wicks, and Drummond Pike, who shared their stories and business; they are an inspiration. The good people at Hollyhock, like Dana Bass Solomon, and some of the "share givers," Shivon Robinson, Rex Weyler, Charles Steinberg and Torkin Wakefield, Rick Ingrasci, and Peggy Taylor, as well as the good Schwartz friends, Eduardo, Gloria, Roberto, and Patricia, helped me as I expanded my vision. As have my teachers along the way, including Reta Lawler, Thomas Huffman, Don Américo Yábar, Kenneth Robinson, and Mary Gormley. Early and late local political connections, from Bill Purcell, Stewart Clifton, Betty Nixon (RIP), Karl Dean, Megan Barry, Colby Sledge, Burkley Allen, and Kristine LaLonde have coached me in the political workings of our neighborhoods. I would like to thank my early and late political connections in Vancouver, including Gregor Robertson and Sadhu Johnston. My Greenways for Nashville friends and cohorts like Shain Dennison, Anne Davis, Emmie Thomas, Elizabeth Mobley, Renee Bates, and Ann Tidwell have taught me how to serve a wonderful organization, so important to leaving a legacy in our city. What is laid down, stays down. My local Urban Land Institute connections from Rose Faeges-Easton, Hunter Gee, Bert Mathews, and Jimmy Granbery are critical. My Vancouver ULI connection Alan Boniface, and of course Ed McMahon at ULI national have expanded my horizons and shaped our policy. I've learned so much from involvement with the Nashville Civic Design Center and from Gary Gaston, Mark Schimmenti, T.K. Davis, and past presidents including Kim Hawkins, Hunter Gee, and Mary Pat Teague. And I would like to thank my Entrepreneurs' Organization Forum 12 mates: Allen Baler, Darek Bell, Max Goldberg, Pete Hermann, Adam James, Bill Kimberlin, and Alan Young, who have given me both business and personal support. Thanks to Stephen Mansfield, who married Sherry and me. And, thanks to my Leadership Nashville class of 2017. Best class ever!

Some of my biggest support has come from my awesome team at Village, like Jenn Garrett, Brian Copeland, James Weinberg (who arrived at Joel's house the same day I did!), Kristy Hairston, Annette Stithem, and Jason Pantana. And of course from Bobbie Noreen, who is always there for me. Newell Anderson, leading the CityLiving Group, and many in my agent ranks, some of the best in the city, have become my friends as we sell and close homes all over the city. I'm grateful for the superstar stalwarts at Village, including Andy Allen, Barbara Moutenot, Virginia Degerberg, Jane Anderson, and Beth Vincent, and to the perennial "top 20," too many to mention. And even to my first two agents, Scott Troxel and Karen Hoff, though they have moved on, as has my first office manager, Marcia Ellenberg. I am ever impressed with the Change Agents at Village, those who are giving to and supporting the work of the Village Fund. And to my great team at Core Development, Andrew Beaird and Kent Campbell, and all of the superstar support at Core and beyond who help us build wonderful communities. And I'd like to give a shout-out to others on my board of directors, including Aaron White and Brad Stevens and to our long-term attorney Doug Kirk, who keeps me out of trouble. And, of course to my board chair Elizabeth Crook, who also oversees all strategic planning work. And to Mike Nolen, who is the best business broker in the world, for his support for Sherry and LetterLogic, and now for me, as we think about ESOPs. Together we have created a wonderful culture and internal community that is making a difference.

Hats off to the Scattered Showers, my band of brothers for so many years, from Sweet Little Tim Buppert, to Myles Maillie, to Robert Fitters, to Marc Rossi, Leroy Bryant, Danny Johnston, Ray Settle, Sherrill Blackman, Steve West, and Village agent Robert Diehl. And to some of those Showers who've gone before us, coach Tim Campbell, Danny Petraitis, Tom Robb, and Danny Rhodes. And of course to the many jugglers whom I've thrown with through the years, including Jeff Raz, my first juggling teacher in Berkeley; Dave Johnson in Arcata; Graham Ellis of Jugglers for Peace in Nicaragua and the Big Island; Jeff Jacobsen, who was also my connection with the orcas; and Nashville Juggling Club members Rebel and Jody Bailey, Laura Novick, Dan Meyer, and Jacob Weiss.

And of course I acknowledge my family, first and foremost my wife, my loving and supportive wife, Sherry Stewart Deutschmann. MFEO baby! Sherry and I have a thing, something that she learned along the way: When one of us offers unsolicited advice, the other can just respond with a "thank you." That is a signal that we were just asking for support, not advice. This, I think, is a good practice for entrepreneurial couples, when both like to "fix" things quickly.

To my father, William Markert Deutschmann, who left me too early, and to my mother, Suzanne, who dazzles us with her wit and political acumen. Love and honor to my grandfather, Robert Sylvester Graetz, and gratitude for his December 31st birthday, and to the many other ancestors who have come before me. And love and respect to my uncle and aunt, Robert and Jeannie Graetz, who have instilled me in civil rights and who are still leaders down in Montgomery today. To the early "extended" family at the Homewood House. To my daughter, Chelsea Gifford, who lends support and youthful wisdom from wherever she is in the world, and to her mother and my ex, K-Lea. And to all of the local family, including my sister, Maggie, my nieces and nephews Daniel, Michelle, and Joy, Sherry's daughter Whitney, and all of their kids—Nikko, Reagan, Anthony, Rocco, and Hayden. I'd like to give a shout-out to my granddaughter Nikko, who has been around since I first started courting her grandmother, who at three years old called Village "Willage," and who picked up on the showmanship of the juggling, now her own show woman with super skill as a hula-hoopster. And of course, I must applaud our personal assistant, Scott Gray; the whole Nashville family could not operate without him.

I'd like to thank my publisher Advantage Media Group and especially Scott Neville. And thanks to Suzanne Kingsbury who lent her shared editing and support to the manuscript. Also to Chris Green and Beverly Mansfield, who read the early version and asked for more; to Anna Hollingsworth, who lent organizational advice; and to Peter Hermann, of my Forum 12 in EO, who gave it a late look with a critical eye.